ALBUM OF
North American
Birds

Matt Vetto

232-2271

ALBUM OF
North American
Birds

Illustrated by CLARK BRONSON
Text by VERA DUGDALE

RAND McNALLY & COMPANY

CHICAGO · NEW YORK · SAN FRANCISCO

Foreword

FROM the earliest times of recorded history, men have been fascinated by the beauty and mystery of birds. Somehow, birds have seemed to be set apart from the rest of the animal kingdom by their power of flight, their gift of song, and their beauty of plumage. They have been symbols of peace, of nobility and courage, of joy and hope. Men have long studied them, and often birds have been linked with omens of good or ill. The owl, with his stately mien, has through the ages been considered a symbol of wisdom, but owing to his habit of night prowling and his ominous hooting call, he has also been considered a bearer of bad tidings and a consort of witches. The stork, which frequently roosts on chimneys or rooftops in Central Europe, is thought to be a symbol of good fortune; but the raven, perhaps because of his somber black plumage, has become a portent of evil.

There is probably no other group of animals to which human attributes have been applied so freely. We speak of the faithfulness of a pair of eagles that mate for life; of the love notes of a male songbird serenading his mate; of the protective care of the helpless young by doting parents; of the cleverness of the mother grouse in feigning a broken wing to distract attention from her nest. Scientists may proclaim that most of this behavior is simply the result of instincts controlled by biological time clocks that set off these actions at appropriate times. But the amateur bird student and bird lover will continue to equate these performances with those of men.

When our nation was young, the flocks of birds on this continent seemed limitless, and little thought was given to protecting them. Awareness of the dangers threatening the survival of many species began to develop about the turn of the century, and since that time important legislation has been passed that has arrested the destruction of many valuable birds. The migratory bird treaties entered into jointly by Canada, the United States, and Mexico have helped materially in the conservation and control of many species. The establishment of numerous well-placed sanctuaries and preserves by governmental and private organizations has also been a valuable factor in bird protection.

Yet there are forces operating against the natural populations of birds that are sometimes subtle and difficult to control. The expansion of housing projects and industry into rural areas, the building of landing fields, the construction of freeways and other types of roads, and the drainage of swamplands are all relatively new developments that have destroyed many of the natural habitats of birds. The wanton killing of numerous hawks, eagles, and other larger species by irresponsible marksmen still continues and is difficult to control, particularly in the wide-open spaces of the West. The recent widespread use of insecticides with their possible effect on birds and other wildlife presents a new problem and needs to be studied with scientific care. But the greater awareness of the need for bird conservation and public concern with it is an encouraging sign.

Of all kinds of living creatures, birds have perhaps been most completely adopted by the amateur, who goes out with his enthusiasm and binoculars to study the habits of these fascinating creatures and with an everlasting hope that he may add yet another species to his life list. Over the years innumerable books have been written about birds. Many of these have been composed by amateurs, which does not mean, however, that they are not authentic, for some of our more accomplished ornithologists have had little formal training in this field. And in spite of the vast literature on birds, there can never be too much written or painted on this subject when it is done with sincerity and accuracy.

Mrs. Dugdale in her short sketches of many of the best-known North American birds conveys a fund of interesting information which will appeal to readers young and old. Mr. Bronson, a wildlife illustrator of unusual accomplishment, has brought to life with careful accuracy the fifty-two species included in the album. The attractive format and style of this book should appeal to a large segment of the general public which may include many who have had no interest in birds before. If it contributes to a more widespread awareness and appreciation of birds in particular and man's natural environment in general it will have performed a most important function. An interest in wildlife by the public is the basis of sound conservation in practice, and without it no state or national legislation can be very effective. The combination of pen and brush of these two artists has produced a work on birds that will be thoroughly enjoyed by many.

C. Lynn Hayward, Ph.D.
DEPARTMENT OF ZOOLOGY
BRIGHAM YOUNG UNIVERSITY

Contents

Bald Eagle

KING of the Birds" is the popular title for the majestic Bald Eagle, long the symbol of liberty and freedom in the United States. Strong, dignified, and imposing in appearance, he seems to typify a fierce spirit of independence, and he is native only to North America. In 1782, the Continental Congress, seeking for a National Emblem, chose the bald eagle. At that time the bird was a familiar sight in every part of the country, where conditions were favorable, from Alaska south through Canada and the United States. But although it was our chosen national bird, it was not until 1940 that the bald eagle was given legal protection. By that time, so many had been destroyed by hunters that they were in danger of becoming extinct. Today, according to a recent survey, there are probably less than 4,000 bald eagles surviving in North America, and the average person has never seen one of these great birds in the wild state.

Haliaeetus leucocephalus leucocephalus is the scientific name of the American bald eagle. A larger species, living chiefly in Alaska and Canada, is known as the northern bald eagle, or *H. leucocephalus alascanus*. The common name of "bald eagle" was given, not because the bird is bald, but because a tight hood of white feathers makes the head appear bare.

Since they are fish eaters, bald eagles live mainly along rivers, lakes, or other bodies of water. Some fish they catch for themselves; some they bully from the osprey (see p. 14). Wounded waterfowl and carrion also form a part of their diet. Monogamous by nature, many eagles hunt and nest with the same mate year after year. Some become wanderers after the nesting season and travel far from their birthplaces.

Eagles mate as warm weather creeps northward; in the South the mating season is February, in the Far North as late as April. The eyrie they build is a massive structure, assembled in the crotch of a tall tree or on a rocky ledge of a vertical cliff, usually near rivers or overlooking the ocean. Branches and sticks are added from year to year until the nest may reach a width of seven feet and contain a ton of materials. This is not so large when one considers the size of the eagle and the fact that the nest is used as a cradle and gymnasium for the young birds, as well as a dining table and a landing strip.

Bald Eagle
1/4 life size
(30-35 in.)

From surprisingly small white eggs, less than three inches in length, one or two downy eaglets hatch. At two weeks the white down is replaced by thick gray wool which in turn is pushed out by dark juvenile feathers when the birds are nine weeks old. For the first few weeks the baby eagles are fed from the mother's beak. Soon they listen for her harsh, broken scream, *"Cac-cac-cac,"* which tells them she is approaching with food. Expectantly they raise their heads and eagerly wait to grasp the prey and tear it to pieces with sharp talons and scythelike beaks.

While the adults hunt or roost on a dry limb or cliff not far from the eyrie, the young birds preen and dress their feathers. They hop up and down on the edge of the platform, stretch their wings, and venture out of the nest briefly. In twelve weeks they leave the nest in wavering flights.

Three to four years pass before the black juveniles acquire the mature plumage and size of an adult. When grown, the male eagle weighs up to eight pounds and has a wingspread of about seven feet. The back and wing plumage may be dark brown with silvery tips or a burnished brown, but his most distinguishing marks are the pure white head and tail which add to his regal appearance.

Golden Eagle

THE PLAINS Indians of long ago sought the Golden Eagle as powerful medicine. The bird was used in many ceremonial rites. In the warbonnets of the bravest warriors, eagle feathers told of valorous deeds. Trapping a live eagle was no mean feat, and one feather might be allowed for this act alone.

The golden eagle is known by many names. Mountain Eagle, War Eagle, Gray Eagle, and Royal Eagle are some of his local titles. *Aquila chrysaëtos* is his Latin name, meaning "golden eagle."

Next to the California condor (see p. 16), the golden eagle is the largest American bird of prey, with a wingspread of six and one-half to seven and one-half feet. Some people consider him an even nobler and handsomer bird than the bald eagle. His plumage is dark brown, becoming almost black on the wings and back, and his name is derived from the golden wash on the back of the head and nape of the neck. The tail is partly white, with a broad black band. His legs are feathered clear to the yellow feet, which in turn are armed with long, curved talons. His slightly larger size and uniform coloring distinguish this eagle from the bald species. The immature bald eagle, before it develops the distinctive white head and tail plumage, is often mistaken for the golden eagle.

The female is slightly larger than the male. Occasionally the well-fed young are larger than the parents when they leave the nest. Once self-supporting and on the wing, they become trim and muscular. If allowed to roam free and unmolested, this handsome bird may live as long as thirty years.

It would be impossible to conceal a nest as large as that required by the golden eagle. The eyrie is found in the top of isolated trees or on shelves of rocky cliffs. Always the nest is high enough from the ground for protection from predators and far enough below the mesas to insure safety from above. The birds return every year to the same site, adding more material to the nest each season.

The golden eagle lays usually two or three white eggs, marked with brown or sienna. It may be true that when the eggs are hatched several days apart, the older and stronger eaglet becomes aggressive, demanding all the parents' attention until the weaker one dies of starvation or is forced from the nest.

The fierce, bold hunter and his mate claim a territory, then defend it against all intruders. Unlike the bald eagle, which always lives near water and whose food is chiefly fish, the golden eagles make their home in mountainous or desert regions and are hunters of small game. Although they may eat carrion, live prey is much more to their liking. Nearly always they hunt from great heights, and their extraordinarily keen eyesight enables them to spot prey from great distances. With deadly talons designed especially for hunting, they swoop down on rabbits, ground squirrels, rats, game birds, songsters, domestic fowl, and now and then a new-born lamb or fawn. Since it is impossible for them to carry a load weighing more than four pounds into the air, they sometimes eat on the ground.

The golden eagle is found in ever-diminishing numbers in Alaska and south to Mexico. It is rarely seen in the east or as far south as Florida. Unless given strict protection, the golden eagle may well disappear from the American continent.

Red-tailed Hawk

IT TAKES a big bundle of sticks to build a nest for the Red-tailed Hawk. Much time and effort must be spent in carrying the heap to a fork in a tree, high above the earth, or in some cranny of a cliff. From the ground it may look like a heap of rubble. But when lined with moss, bark, lichens, leaves, and twigs, it makes a perfect place for Mother Hawk to lay two, or sometimes three, white eggs, lightly splashed with brownish purple.

While Mother Hawk attends to her brooding duties, Father Hawk finds it profitable to perch on a limb where he can closely observe the floor of the woods or desert below. His chocolate brown coat, mottled with white or gray and the lighter underparts streaked with brown, blends with his surroundings. Small creatures may not see the silent sentinel, but the keen eyes of the hawk quickly spy the slightest movement in the grass or leaves. Before a scurrying squirrel hears the swish of wings, long, curved talons close about him. Many mice, squirrels, gophers, prairie dogs, and snakes, along with heaps of grasshoppers and beetles, find their way to the nest of the red-tail.

Some people call the red-tailed hawk a chicken thief, but he rarely preys on barnyard fowl when other game is available. On the other hand, the destruction he does among harmful rodents is of great service to the farmer.

Baby hawks are weak and blind when they are hatched. The light covering of white down is soon replaced by dark brownish-gray feathers of the juvenile. Both parents provide food for the hungry young, and on the bountiful supply they soon become active and sassy. They squawk and screech and quarrel among themselves, snatching morsels of meat from the curved, strong beaks of their nest-mates. When they leave the nest their cry is a shrill *"Kree-e-e-e, kree-e-e-e."* Then we know the red-tail is on the wing.

High above the earth the red-tailed hawk soars in wide circles. When he sees a prospective meal far below, he folds his wings and nose-dives toward the earth. Just in the nick of time, the wide wings are spread, the tail fanned, and he comes in for a perfect landing, talons ready for seizing the prey.

At other times the hawks skim above the rocky hillsides and brush-covered slopes. They love deep pine forests and heavily wooded areas, but are also found in

Red-tailed Hawk
1/4 life size
(19-24 in.)

plains and deserts. Wherever they are seen they are a target for the farmer's gun, because of their undeserved reputation as chicken thieves. At one time, great flights of red-tailed hawks were observed on their annual migrations in spring and fall. Now they are seldom seen in many localities. Protection by law may preserve the ones we still have with us.

The red-tailed hawk (*Buteo jamaicensis*) is one of the largest and most widely distributed members of the hawk family. Altogether, six subspecies are scattered throughout North America from Alaska to Mexico and Florida, and from east to west across the continent.

If you would know the red-tailed hawk, remember the female is larger than the male, with a wingspread up to fifty inches, measuring up to twenty-five inches in length and weighing three pounds. In flight the hawk's wings appear broad and round, and the flight is slow. The most characteristic mark of the male is the brick-red coloring on the upper side of the fan-shaped tail, usually with a distinct black bar near the end, which gives him the name of red-tail.

Osprey

INDUSTRIOUS fisherman that he is, the Osprey is on the wing from morning 'till night. He has much fishing to do. He not only fishes for himself, his mate, and young, but occasionally—and unintentionally—for the bald eagle and tern.

"*Kyeek! Kyeek! Kyeek!*" cries the osprey. "A fish! A fish!" And dives to seize it.

From a promontory overlooking the fishing waters, an eagle spies the successful catch. Down he swoops. The osprey dives and darts in an effort to evade his tormentor. Burdened with the extra weight of the fish, he tires soon and is forced to drop his prize. Swift as a dart, the eagle catches the fish in midair and flies back to his perch to dine.

Back to his endless fishing the osprey must go, tirelessly skimming above the water on long, narrow-angled wings. The keen eyes search for another fish; then down he plunges, striking for the fish with his taloned feet. Sometimes he seems barely to touch the surface; sometimes he sends a spray of water cascading about him as he completely submerges. He rises to the surface and shakes his hard, close, well-oiled plumage. Grasping the slippery fish in sharp black talons, the osprey wings to his own retreat.

During the days of courtship, the ospreys have a high-flying time. The mating pair soar high in the sky, dive in short free falls, and play tag.

The very tip-top of an isolated tree is the perfect place for an osprey's nest, although nests have been found under bridges, in towers, among cliffs, and on rocky inclines along the seashore. In some areas ospreys nest close to inhabited areas, too, and their nests have been seen on the ground in marshy lowlands and along large rivers.

The first nest of the osprey and his life-long mate is modest. It is built of sticks, reeds, bones, and seaweed, and softly lined with grass. Each year the osprey family adds a bit more building material—a stick here, a piece of driftwood there—until it becomes quite an imposing structure.

Two to four reddish-brown-splashed eggs are laid by the female. She patiently broods for thirty-five days. Then she feeds the baby birds from her own beak until they are old enough to tear their own food to bits. Both parents supply fish as they grow. At eight to ten weeks the fledglings try their wings.

The juvenile covering gradually turns from its general protective coloring to the plumage of an adult. The head and neck are sleek and white, somewhat like that of the bald eagle, marked with brownish-black and yellowish at the nape. The head feathers can be erected in a short crest. The underparts and breast are white, lightly touched with brown, and the upper parts are reddish-brown frosted with white. The thighs are covered with short, tight feathers, the lower leg with bluish-yellow scales. An adult will measure about two feet in length, with a wingspread of four and one-half to five and one-half feet.

The osprey (*Pandion haliaetus*) or the fish hawk, has disappeared from many of his inland haunts. He is still seen in decreasing numbers along our Pacific and Atlantic shorelines, from Alaska to the Gulf of Mexico. Inhabitants of the Far North migrate to the tropics in the winter, while the southern ospreys remain in the same areas throughout the year.

California Condor

IN A REMOTE mountainous area of the Los Padres National Forest in southern California, a refuge has been established for one of our rarest birds, the California Condor.

Once this great black bird of prey was numerous in the southern part of the United States. Bones and fossils dating back to the Pleistocene epoch have been found in Texas and Florida. Scientists believe that the condors once fed on the carcasses of prehistoric monsters. Ancient Indian tribes of North America worshiped the condor as the sacred thunderbird. Early explorers saw them feeding on the remains of dead whales washed ashore on the seacoast, and observed them on their flyway from Mexico to the Columbia River region. Now not more than seventy condors (*Gymnogyps californianus*) are sheltered in their inland retreat.

An adult condor may weigh as much as a large turkey and stand three to four feet tall. On the ground condors are rather awkward, walking on large feet, with toes little adapted to taking live prey. High plateaus and ridges are favored as feeding places. Here the condor can hurl himself from a cliff and be immediately airborne. On widespread wings, measuring up to ten and one-half feet, he rides the prevailing air currents high above the clouds, or circles over the landscape, keen eyes searching for a morsel of food below. The carcasses of large game animals or domestic livestock make a desirable dinner, but even small bits of decaying matter are never bypassed.

One condor dropping to earth seems to be the signal for all others for miles around to gather for a feast. They fold their wings like black capes, perch on the carcass and tear the hide with thick, curved beaks. They squabble over tender morsels. The heads, neck, and crop of the adult birds are reddish orange, naked except for a sparse covering of hairlike feathers. The underwings are white. Scattered through the crowd are a few smaller birds, all rusty black. These are juveniles who have not attained full plumage. Not until they are five to six years of age and ready to mate will they show the red coloring of the eye and the orange head.

Condors are said to mate only once and for life. Each pair nests only every other year. Early in the spring the nesters retire to a rocky ledge, high on an inaccessible mountain. Here on a bare floor among rocks and boulders the female

California Condor
1/7 life size
(45-55 in.)

lays a single greenish-white egg. It takes forty-eight days for the egg to hatch. The young bird remains at the nesting site for about twenty weeks before it ventures abroad. It is seven months old before it takes to the air and is able to forage for itself. During this long period the parents feed the young bird by regurgitation with gentle, affectionate care. Each day they fly many miles in search of food.

Wary and shy, the condor resents any intrusion into his breeding and nesting grounds. Observers believe that not more than five young birds reach the age of maturity each year. For this reason conservationists now forbid entry to the sanctuary during the spring and summer. The law forbids men to shoot them. But there are many other hazards, since they travel far from their refuge each day.

National, state, and local agencies have combined their efforts to save this rare bird from extinction. Individuals should share the responsibility for saving our largest living bird capable of flight.

Turkey Vulture

BUZZARDS are circling overhead. Stopping to watch them for a moment, one looks about for something dead or dying. The ominous birds swoop down from the sky. They are descending for a meal.

It is a surprise to learn that this bird we call a buzzard is not a buzzard at all. This title is rightfully reserved for a certain one of the hawk family. But in some localities the Turkey Vulture has become so well known as the Turkey Buzzard that it is doubtful if he will ever be called by any other name. *Cathartes aura* is the scientific name for this vulture. It is particularly fitting, too, for *Cathartes* means purifier. The turkey vulture is one of nature's most effective scavengers.

In the South, this bird of prey shares the skies with a close relative, the black vulture. His range, however, is much wider, extending north to British Columbia, and across the western part of the United States. He is partial to the open prairies and barren mountains of the West, the deserts of the South and Southwest, and swamps. Along the Pacific Coast he feeds on dead fish and sea animals he finds along the shores. Carcasses of cattle, sheep, game animals, and rodents are the object of search on the island. He visits city dumps or feeds on dead rabbits and other animals along our highways. The turkey vulture is not a shy bird, but he does move aside for oncoming traffic to pass. Then he returns to his cleanup work.

The flight of the vulture is a thing of beauty. Few other birds have such mastery of flight. With a wingspread of six feet, he circles slowly, serenely, taking advantage of the slightest whim of the air currents and crosswinds to keep aloft. The lighter flight feathers and gray underwings are plainly visible when he is in flight. Wings perceptibly raised above the horizontal tells us this is neither eagle, osprey, nor raven.

On the ground the vulture presents a more somber picture. He stands two and one-half feet tall. His small red head is ugly, wrinkled, and bare. The horn-colored beak is thick and blunt. The feet and toes are pink, lacking the sharp talons necessary for taking live prey. The plumage is rusty black, rough and unkempt. The lower neck and back feathers show a purple sheen. Piercing eyes are lined with yellow. Like a black shroud, the wings fold about the hunched body, reaching well beyond the tail.

The turkey vulture is a lazy bird. He spends the morning hours stretching his wings in the sun. At dusk he flies to a bare limb on a dead tree. It takes much wing-flapping and awkward limb-walking to find a suitable roost. A grunt or hiss of disapproval is the only voice he possesses.

The female does not build a nest but lays her single egg in a hollow log, a cave, or a depression in the ground. From egg to yellow hatchling to dusky juvenile, the young bird is completely dependent on the parents for food. During the nesting period the father is the willing provider. Later, both parents feed the young one by regurgitation.

It is doubtful if the turkey vulture ever attacks live animals or birds. It has no natural enemies. Most men recognize the importance of the work the vulture performs, and even those who commonly use other birds for targets seem to obey the unwritten law, that the turkey vulture is unfair game.

Great Horned Owl

DRESSED in a mottled coat of tawny brown and russet tan, with a white neck-piece tucked neatly inside a black-and-white barred vest, the Great Horned Owl (*Bubo virginianus*) blends with the shadows of his forest haunts. At dusk the deadly hunter spreads his wings and glides over fields and meadows, through thickets and woods, in his nightly search for food. The yellow eyes glow like amber foglights in the dark. No whir of wings alerts the unsuspecting prey to the shadowy approach of certain death. With tail down, powerful feet and talons thrust forward in a grasping position, the owl swoops down for the kill. The hooked beak, strong as steel and sharp as a cutlass, tears a hapless rabbit or grouse into bite-size pieces. A mouse, mole, or smaller tidbit is swallowed whole.

At dawn the owl retreats to a dark roosting spot. Perched on a limb with wings folded close to his body, the round head topped with two-inch feather tufts which resemble ears or horns, the owl looks like a fence-sitting cat. His deep, hooting call ("*Hoo, hoo-oo, hoo, hoo*") carries a threat and defiance to all who hear it.

It takes a long time to rear a family of owlets, so the great horned owl begins early in the year. In January and February, or as late as March in the North, the male calls to the female with a resonant hoot. The female is larger than the male. She sometimes reaches a body length of twenty-two to twenty-four inches, with a wingspread up to fifty inches. To impress her, the male does a strange courtship dance. He bobs. He bows. He ruffles up his feathers and hops about with an important air. He flutters from limb to limb and makes flying sorties into the air. Sometimes he returns with an offering of food. They share the repast, after which she joins the dance, hopping and bobbing about as though keeping time to the beat of an inner drum.

Owls are poor home builders. They prefer to nest in a large hollow in a tree or even to occupy the deserted nest of a hawk or crow. These structures are large and rough, built of sticks and bark and lined with leaves or feathers. Sometimes owls nest on a rocky ledge, or even on the bare ground.

The mother lays two or three round, dull white eggs. Then she stoically

Great Horned Owl
1/3 life size
(18-24 in.)

settles herself on the nest and spreads her feather skirts about her to protect her precious charges from snow and cold.

It is five weeks before the first downy white owlet pecks its way out of the shell. As the young birds feather out, they look like wise old men with their wide eyes and quizzical expressions. They clamor for food and keep the parents busy supplying mice, squirrels, rabbits, crayfish, and beetles. Later in the season baby crows are taken. Migrating songsters, waterfowl, and game birds all fall prey to the hungry family. It is nearly ten weeks before fledglings leave the nest to search for their own food. The parent birds weary of family life by November, and drive the young owls away to establish hunting ranges of their own.

Where there is an abundance of rodents and other food, the great horned owl remains in the same locality year after year. In the Far North he may be forced to migrate short distances in search of game. He is widely distributed through the United States, Canada, and south central Alaska.

Although he is considered one of the most bloodthirsty and daring birds of prey, the great horned owl also performs an important service to man by keeping rodent populations in check.

Barn Owl

THE BARN OWL is a faithful night watchman. He spends his days dozing in a dark retreat, but when night comes he is wide awake and on the wing. Silent as a ghost he patrols farmyards, meadows, the fringes of woodlots, and outbuildings. Because one of his favorite haunts happens to be a dark barn, he is widely known as the barn owl.

The nest of the barn owl is found in hollow trees, holes in steep banks, caves, burrows in the ground, tucked in a corner of a musty loft or church steeple, or anyplace where mice are plentiful. He eats mice for breakfast, mice for lunch, and mice for dinner.

The female lays five to seven white eggs in a rough nest. Both parents take turns keeping the eggs warm. It is not unusual to see the father sitting on the nest while the mother bird is away hunting.

Baby owls hatch in five weeks. They look like white balls of fuzz, with feet and beak projecting. In a few days their coats turn buff; their eyes are now their most prominent feature. The parent birds probably think they are all mouths, for the young birds have such big appetites that it keeps the parents busy carrying mice, gophers, moles, beetles, and grasshoppers to them.

As soon as the young develop juvenile feathers, they leave the nest and learn to hunt for their own food. The parent birds hurry them along, for a pair of owls often have two families each year.

The barn owl frequently reaches a length of eighteen inches, with a wing-spread of almost four feet. The plumage is light but protective. The breast is white or tawny buff, generously splattered with dark dots. The wings and back are darker with an overlay of mottled gray and black or brown. The legs are long and slender, lightly feathered, and bent in at the knee joints, thus giving him that "knock-kneed" appearance. Small, dark eyes peer from a white, round, or heart-shaped facial disk. The fine feathers which make up the disk and the stiff, hairlike bristles which almost conceal the long beak are thought to be sound sensitive. They may aid the owl in striking prey in total darkness. The eyes of the owl are night seeing. They gather light, making it possible for him to see much better in the dark than he does in bright sunlight.

The voice of the barn owl is a quavering, querulous cry. If he is molested on his roost, he scolds peevishly, fluffs his feathers like a puffball, spreads his wings wide, and hisses and snaps his bill. The round head swings from side to side and up and down as though moving on a swivel. He cannot move his eyes, so he must move his head to see all that goes on about him.

Tyto alba, the barn owl, has representatives in nearly all parts of the world. In the United States he is one of the best-known members of the owl family. He is seen in almost every state, although rare in the intermountain West, and as far north as the western coastal areas of British Columbia.

The barn owl never preys on domestic poultry. In fact, he is one of the farmer's best friends. It is said that he eats his weight in rodents every night. And in return for his services, he asks nothing more than a spot where he may nest unmolested, or the safety of a roost in a dark barn.

Wild Turkey

THERE is a stir of springtime activity in the woods. This is the time when the Wild Turkey, weary of bachelorhood, goes a-courting. He is dressed in a handsome bronze suit which gleams in ever-changing colors from blue to green and brownish purple. The square-cut feathers enfold the sleek body like an armor of metallic scales. He spreads his black-tipped tail in a wide fan, and droops his wings to the ground. Bright eyes peer from the slender, red-blue head. Bright red wattles hang at the base of the neck. With a tassel dangling from his breast, the puffed-up dandy gobbles his strange love call.

The smaller hens, dressed in drab plumage and without the breast adornment, slip shyly from the woods to see what all the racket is about. The gobbler loses no time in appointing himself Lord Protector of several hens and defending his title against any challenger. With a flourish of spurs and beaks, the sparring males send feathers and blood flying. To the victor goes the harem, and meekly the hens submit to his rule.

Early in the morning a hen steals away from the flock. In a nest hidden deep in a thicket she lays each day a large speckled egg. Warily she comes and goes, watching for the crow, the raccoon, opossum, and other predators. One morning she does not return to her master, but remains quietly on the nest. In twenty-eight days, from eight to fifteen downy heads form a circle beneath her wings. With slow, deliberate steps she guides the new brood into the woods. She clucks softly to reassure them. She knows where mast is deepest beneath the nut-bearing trees. She knows where to scratch in moldering leaves to turn insects and seeds to light. Almost at once the little ones are busy scratching for themselves. In two weeks they are feathered and can fly to an overhanging limb. They spread out on either side of the mother to roost. Here they are fairly safe from predators, but they make a good target for moonlight poachers.

By fall the young birds are as large as their mother. They have become fat on berries, acorns, nuts, and the grain they sometimes glean from fields near the woods. They are timid and wary. The snap of a twig sends them running swiftly and quietly to cover.

The wild turkey is our largest game bird. Large "Toms" often weigh thirty

Wild Turkey
1/6 life size
(48 in.)

pounds or more and may be four feet in length. It was the wild turkey (*Meleagris gallopavo silvestris*) that the early colonists found in the eastern and southern woods. It was on the table at the first Thanksgiving feast. It became the ancestor of our traditional festive bird, by a rather devious route. Spanish explorers introduced the Mexican species, domesticated by the Aztecs, into Spain in the sixteenth century. From there it spread over Europe, and eventually found its way back to America. Our domesticated turkey today is larger and tamer, but it has lost much of the natural charm of the wild turkey.

Now the wild turkeys have vanished from many old retreats. Poaching and destruction of their natural habitat have depleted their numbers. The southern states are the stronghold of the largest flocks, but they have also been introduced to many western states where they have adapted themselves to new surroundings.

Brushy, wooded swamps and bottomlands, piñon forests, groves of hardwood, brakes, and chaparral thickets near water in the Southwest are places where they thrive. Allowed to remain here and given stringent protection, the wild turkey can still be ours.

Sage Grouse

HAVE you ever stood on a hill at twilight, surrounded by a sea of blue-gray sage, to be suddenly startled by a gray-brown feathered bomb exploding at your feet? Did you hear the whir of wings, the cackle of alarm? And did you mark the spot, and hurry there, only to find the quarry had vanished? This was the Sage Grouse (*Centrocercus urophasianus*), also called the Sage Hen. Next to the wild turkey, it is our largest game bird. It is the largest member of the grouse family and in some ways is unique.

The mating habits of the sage grouse are remarkable. In early spring, flocks of sage cocks gather in open terrain. Their rather drab plumage is varied with white, black, brown, and yellow. A black collar and black underparts are separated by a snow-white breast. The heavy bodies and long sharp tails distinguish this bird from other grouse.

The male chooses a partner at random. He spreads his spearlike tail feathers in a splendid fan. He drops his wings and fluffs his plumage. Bare, yellow sacs at the sides of the head are inflated and deflated, making queer popping noises. He dances about his chosen lady, expanding his breast and pushing it on the ground before him until it becomes ragged by the end of the mating season.

The smaller hens make their nests on sunny slopes near streams. Under a sagebush or in a clump of grass, well concealed, the hen lays eight to thirteen buff-and-brown-spotted eggs. A few minutes after the peeping chicks hatch they are busy scratching for seeds and insects.

The first two weeks are most hazardous for the young birds. A hard rain or hailstorm, along with predators, may take a heavy toll. Coyotes are by far their most dangerous enemy. Mother Hen has learned to deal with this pesky fellow. She cries pitifully and limps away dragging a wing. When the hungry coyote has been lured far afield, she suddenly recovers, makes a wide detour, and is soon back with her family. The roosters remain apart, taking no part in rearing the young birds.

The food of the sage grouse consists mainly of the leaves of the sagebrush, especially in winter, together with some insects. During the summer the sage grouse visit farms. In return for destroying many insects and grasshoppers, they may filch alfalfa and sweet clover seeds, as well as various grains.

By fall the young birds are as large as the adults, lighter in color, but weighing up to two or four pounds and measuring twenty to thirty inches in length. As winter approaches, they gather in large flocks. On cold days they huddle together for warmth, forming a circle with the tails in and the heads out. When the sagebrush is covered with snow, they migrate to open woods to feed. Dressed in warm down and feathered stockings, the hardy birds ignore the cold.

As the name implies, the sage grouse belongs to the sagebrush-covered lands of the West, preferably where there are small streams and springs. From British Columbia through the Rocky Mountain states, the Great Basin, and south to Mexico, wherever there are still large tracts of sagebrush, the sage grouse is seen. But with the destruction of the sagebrush, and with indiscriminate hunting, the sage grouse has dwindled in numbers. With proper protection, it could once more thrive in areas close to civilization and become quite numerous in places where it is not molested.

Ring-necked Pheasant

THE PHEASANT is not a native American bird, and the Ring-necked Pheasant, as we know him, is a blending of several subspecies. Developed over a period of years, from imported Chinese, Mongolian, and European stock, the ringneck (*Phasianus colchicus*) has taken to his land of adoption so well that he is no longer considered an alien. Unsuccessful attempts were made to introduce English and ring-necked pheasants to America as early as the eighteenth century. In 1880 the pheasants were successfully imported to Oregon, and since that time they have been widely distributed through the United States and southern Canada. This pheasant is one of our most beautiful game birds.

If there is a pheasant rooster in the neighborhood, he can be identified by his fowl-like manners and his plumage. His is a coat of the finest burnished hues. The long, pointed tail of golden brown marked with bars of dark brown is his most distinguishing feature. The head shines with a blue-green sheen. A red eye-patch surrounds the eye. The body shades from yellow buff to golden brown, decorated with black-and-white-tipped feathers. Old Ringneck gets his name from the white collar he wears.

In spring the arrogant male stretches on his toes, flaps his wings, and crows. Several small, mottled brown hens remain near him through the mating and laying season. An invading rooster with a roving eye should be prepared for battle. Strong wings, stout beaks, and legs armed with spurs equip the males to fight until one or the other takes a sound beating.

The hen makes her nest in tall weeds or hay at the edge of fields, along ditch banks, in hedgerows, thickets, and bushes. So long as the undergrowth is at least six inches tall, she can bury herself and remain unseen.

Although she may lay a dozen eggs, the hen often comes off the nest with fewer chicks. Raccoons, weasels, opossums, skunks, and dogs sometimes destroy the nests and scatter the young. When this happens, the hen lays more eggs and remains on the nest for another twenty-three days.

The young birds remain with the mother during the summer. By fall they are grown. They weigh one to three pounds, spread their wings for thirty-two inches, and measure thirty or more inches in length.

Ring-necked Pheasant
1/4 life size
(32-36 in.)

Pheasants gather in small flocks as winter approaches. On cold days they feed in a restricted area and roost on the ground. When the weather is warm they scatter, feeding on windswept slopes or in protected ravines. They scour old grain patches and cornfields. Under nut-bearing trees they find nuts, dry berries, and seeds. Green vegetation by open springs attracts them. Insects are never bypassed. Where there is sufficient cover and food, they remain on the same range throughout the year.

The pheasant is bold. He is sly. He is swift afoot. He takes to the air with a flurry of wings and a harsh cackle. Even though he is a strong flier, he is much more at home on the ground, and is extremely clever at concealment. When he is in dense cover, a hunter without a dog has little chance of flushing him.

There is little danger the pheasant will disappear from our landscape in the near future. He is too popular with hunters. Game farms produce thousands of birds every year which are released in favorable localities. It is hoped they will mingle with their wild brothers and increase the ringneck population.

American Woodcock

THE WOODCOCK is a member of the long-billed sandpiper family. His local names are many, among them, Timber Doodle, Wood Snipe, Bog Sucker, and Peewee. *Philohela minor,* meaning "swamp bird," is a fitting title. He loves deep swampy woods, thickets, brushy bottomlands, and heavy brush cover. In higher altitudes he is found on boggy hillsides, among willows, alder, and stands of conifer or hardwoods. Always there must be water and rich soil from which to dig great quantities of earthworms.

During the day the woodcock hides in a dense thicket. At nightfall he flies to a favorite feeding ground. He does not wait for the worm to come to him. He goes after the worm with a special tool designed for boring holes in the damp earth. The upper part of the long, slender bill is longer than the lower, and has a movable tip. With this, he hooks the worms. Many holes in the soil indicate that he has eaten well.

The female is larger than the male. Both are clad in protective browns, russet, tans, and black, and so subtle is the coloring that their plumage seems entangled with the deep woodsy tones of the underbrush.

The mating dance of the woodcock is a twilight performance. The male spirals into the sky on whistling wings. Above a clearing, he sings his clear love notes: *"Chicaree, chicaree, chicaree."* On the downward spiral he zigzags and chirps, *"Zeeip, zeeip, zeeip."* He comes to earth in the territory of a female. He is a small, plump-bodied fellow, weighing about eight ounces, and is approximately eleven inches long. Usually quiet and secretive, during the mating season he struts about like a small rooster. He spreads his short tail, droops his wings, thrusts out the speckled chest, and preens to attract the attention of the female.

His mate does not mind that he sings to several other females in the vicinity. She is busy finding a secluded spot to lay four buff-and-russet eggs. As she sits on her ground nest, she resembles a heap of rusty leaves. Round, bright eyes, set high in the large head, enable her to see in nearly a complete circle about her without moving her head. She holds tight to the nest. Only in the face of extreme danger will she flush. Then she flies straight up in a thicket, winging away with such erratic flight that she is gone before a startled observer knows what has happened.

The nesting period is short. The hen sits for twenty-one days. Then for two weeks she stuffs the young birds with worms, larvae of flies and beetles, insects, and as they grow older, seeds and some vegetation. The young birds leave the nest and fly weakly when fourteen days old. At four weeks they can fly and bore for their own worms. During this period, the mother provides an airlift for them. She has been seen flying to and from feeding areas with a young bird held securely against her body with the short, strong legs. It seems she also uses the bill in this operation. She will carry off her young in this way if the nest is disturbed.

The woodcocks leave their homes in southeastern Canada, New Brunswick, Nova Scotia, and the northeastern part of the United States in late fall. They migrate by night, flying low, resting during the day, and feeding in early morning and late evening. Their winter home is in the south central and Gulf states. But as soon as the earth thaws in March and April, they make the long flight back to their summer homes in the North.

Ruffed Grouse

IN EARLY spring the northern woods echo with the roll of muffled drums. The drummer is a male Ruffed Grouse. The drums are his stout wings, and his stage is a log or stump. He struts up and down until he finds the exact spot where he has drummed many times before. There he stands erect, crest raised and head high. A dark blue-green ruff glistens above his shoulders. The handsome black-banded tail is spread in a fan. *Rump, a-rump, ka-thump.* The tempo of the drumming increases until it sounds like the roar of a distant motor. The drumming stops, and the grouse looks about to see if he has an audience.

This is the only voice the grouse has during the mating season. The drumming is a call to the shy hens to come to him, a warning to other males to stay away. It tells the world it is spring, and the ruffed grouse is alive and filled with vigor.

The ruffed grouse is a large, chicken-like bird. There are two phases in America: the red-brown phase of the Pacific West and the gray phase of the inland mountains. The wide, black terminal band on the tail marks the ruffed grouse from other members of the grouse family. The plumage is mottled gray or brown, with buff, white, and brownish markings. The tail is crossed with narrow bands of dark brown or black. Bold bars of dark gray or brown cross the breast. The hens are the same size as the males, weighing nearly two pounds and about eighteen inches long. Their tails are shorter than the male's, and the shoulder ruff is smaller..

The hen hides her nest on the ground in dense undergrowth, or beneath the shelter of a fallen log, or at the base of a tree. She lays eight to fourteen buff eggs. Huddled motionless over her nest, she is invisible. The fox and owl may never see her. If they do, they are greeted by a flurry of angry feathers as she tries to drive them away.

The eggs hatch in twenty-three days. As soon as the downy chicks are dry, the family leaves the nest to search for bugs and insects. At night the babies sleep on the forest floor under the wings of the hen. As soon as they can fly, they roost in trees. During the day they sun themselves and dust their feathers. After the first week, they eat such a variety of food there is little

Ruffed Grouse
1/3 life size
(16-19 in.)

danger of a famine overtaking them. Grubs and insects, seeds, buds of alder, aspen, and nuts from the hardwood forests; acorns, herbs, wild grapes, and apples supply them with food. By autumn they are almost grown.

Bonasa umbellus, as the grouse is known scientifically, is a hardy bird. In winter he is warmly clad in dense feathery down which can be fluffed to form air pockets. Stiff feathers like bristles grow out from the sides of the feet, making fine snowshoes. In bitter cold weather, or when a blizzard rages, the ruffed grouse dives into a snowbank and buries himself beneath a blanket of snow. He is independent, cautious, and solitary.

The ruffed grouse is a popular game bird, but the hunter will seldom surprise him on the ground. Like a whirlwind, he bursts into the air, making a difficult target. Where his habitat has been destroyed, the ruffed grouse has disappeared, but he is still found in wilderness areas of Alaska, Canada, and the northern part of the United States. He thrives in high altitudes. Given proper protection, open woods and forests in which to feed and find shelter, pure water, and a bit of gravel, this brave and wary bird may survive for many years. So drum away, ruffed grouse.

Greater Prairie Chicken

THE PRAIRIE CHICKEN is a fowl of the plains. He lives in tall grass country, and feeds, nests, and finds protection on the open prairie. Prairie Indians of the early days trapped the hens to supply the lodges with sweet, tender meat. White settlers found them, too. They killed them with guns, sticks, and stones, not just for meat, but for sport. The great disaster for the prairie chickens came when men plowed the grasslands, thus destroying their habitat and food. Once numbered in the millions, there are now but a few prairie chickens left, and these in widely scattered areas.

Tympanuchus cupido, the greater prairie chicken, is found from the plains of central Canada south to Colorado, Montana, and Kansas. The Latin name, *Tympanuchus,* means kettledrum. *Cupido* refers to the tufts of stiff feathers that overlay air sacs on the necks of the males. These can be erected like cupid wings, although some say they look like horns.

The "booming" begins in February and continues through May. The roosters come to a knoll in a fairly open place before daybreak. They slip out of the grass, or alight from the air with a noisy cackle. Each male has an area in which to perform his mating dance. They fluff their brown-barred plumage, spread wide the wings and droop them to the ground. They raise the tail and lower the soft, crested heads. Large orange sacs on the heads are inflated. As the air is released, the kettledrum *boom-ah-oohm* carries far across the prairie and attracts the curious hens.

The roosters perform as if answering a square-dance caller. They shuffle forward, stamp the ground, pivot, and halt. As the tempo of the dance increases, one is seen leaping into the air with a loud cackle. Duels between the males are fought with feet, beaks, and wings. The combats seem fierce, but after the competition is over the rivals feed peacefully together.

The little prairie hens are model mothers. They build a grass nest on the ground beneath a canopy of grass and weeds. For more than three weeks they sit on spotted olive eggs. Sometimes they have as many as seventeen chicks to care for and raise by themselves. The busy mothers waste no time in showing their broods where to look for bugs and insects, of which they destroy a great number during the summer months. If an enemy is near, every chick freezes. The mothers cluck softly to tell them when they may come out of hiding. Like all grouse, they grow quickly.

When the young birds are full grown they measure about eighteen inches in length, and weigh from one to two pounds. The roosters are larger than the hens. The neck tufts of the females are shorter, there are no air sacs, and the square tail feathers are barred with buff and brown. The legs are feathered in the front and the toes are webbed at the base. The prairie chicken is a strong flier. He takes to the air with a loud cackle and is gone in graceful flight.

In autumn, when flocks gather, the hens and the young birds join the roaming roosters. Now they feed in fallow fields or in stubble ground. In wild briar patches they find rose hips, dry fruit, and sunflower seeds. Heavy winds, hailstorms, and rain take the lives of many during the winter months.

What a pity it would be if this attractive and popular game bird is allowed to become extinct! But it needs protection from hunters and it also needs the restoration of its natural foods—the prairie flowers and grasses—to survive.

Bobwhite

THIS cheerful friend of the farmer lives where field and meadows meet the woods. His merry whistle delights the hearts of all who hear him. To his mate he whistles soft love notes filled with emotion. To the farmer, he sings of warm days and more rain. *"More-wet, more-wet, more-wet,"* he seems to say. Quail or partridge he has been called, yet he clearly tells his name: *"Bob-bob-white, bobwhite, bobwhite."*

Bobwhite is a plump, chickenlike bird, slightly larger than a meadowlark. He wears a rich coat of brown and buff, the brownest of all the quail. A white line across the face and over the eye and a pure white throat are marks by which the bobwhite is known.

April and May are his months of courtship. Mr. Bobwhite is a bold suitor; the little female, ever shy and coy. He runs by her side to attract her attention. Although he is usually friendly with other males, he has no time now for sociability. Fierce battles often take place between two rivals.

The nest of the bobwhite is woven of dry grass and sheltered in tall weeds or beneath brushy cover. This is where the female lays from ten to twenty white eggs and carefully arranges them with the small end down. Mr. Bobwhite is a kind and constant companion. He shares the sitting duties with his little brown-and-buff mate and is a good provider. Every morning for twenty-three days he sings to her from a thicket or the limb of a tree.

Baby bobwhites are quaint and lively from the moment they hatch. The father joins his family when they leave the nest, and the chicks have his watchful care until they are grown. He proudly scratches in grass and leaves to find insects and seeds for them. His call of alarm sends the babies running to hide beneath their mother's skirts. As soon as the young birds are feathered, the family roosts in a tight circle, tails to the inside and heads facing out. They are constantly on the alert for the fox, hawk, or the owl. They hug the ground until they seem to fade into the earth, becoming practically invisible. When flushed, they burst from the circle like an exploding bombshell and scatter in all directions. Their flight is swift and strong.

The bobwhites have their own private walkways through the underbrush.

Bobwhite
3/5 life size
(8½ -10½ in.)

The babies follow the parents in single file from field to meadow and back to the edge of the woods. During the day they sun themselves and dust their feathers. If an accident befalls the mother, the father is equal to the task of rearing the family by himself. By fall, the young birds are full grown. They have eaten pecks of harmful insects and weed seeds. In the fields they have gleaned corn, rye, wheat, and other grains. Now, they join other families to form a bevy. But more than half the young bobwhites have perished, the victims of many predators, and more will fall to the hunter during the hunting season, for Bobwhite is one of our favorite game birds.

Heavy winter snows force the birds into the woods to feed beneath the pine and nut trees. Because they roost on the ground they are sometimes imprisoned by freezing snow and die of starvation. Yet, they are hardy. Bound by deep ties of affection, they remain together until the spring pairing season.

Although *Colinus virginianus* calls himself bobwhite, he is actually a member of the quail family. He is a resident chiefly of the eastern part of the United States, from Canada to the Gulf, but has also been introduced into Hawaii, British Columbia, Washington, Oregon, and other western states with much success. Here, too, his merry whistle is always welcome.

Mourning Dove

SOME people may think Mourning Doves have nothing to do all day but bill and coo. On the contrary, they are very busy birds. They raise not one, but two or three families in a single season.

In the South mourning doves begin nesting in January and February. Many flocks, however, fly north to a breeding range which extends from Alaska southward through Canada and into the northern part of the United States. As soon as the birds arrive in April and May, their nesting activities begin.

All through the spring and summer, the tender, sorrowful mating song of the mourning dove is heard. *"Coo, coo, coo,"* he sighs mournfully. From these sad notes the mourning dove has been named. Yet this dove is not as unhappy as the name sounds. He makes spectacular mating flights into the air, flapping his wings noisily, and then glides down to perch beside a loving, devoted mate.

Mourning doves are poor home builders, probably because their bills and feet are ill adapted to construction work. Their nest is a small platform of twigs, crudely laced together on horizontal limbs of pines and other trees, or sometimes on the ground. They are fortunate that the two white eggs do not fall through holes in the unlined structure!

Father Dove sits on the nest in the daytime; Mother sits at night. In only thirteen days the scrawny babies hatch. They feed by placing their bills in the throat of a parent where they find "pigeon milk," a predigested food mixed with liquid from the crop. The youngsters quickly feather into ungainly "squabs." In two weeks they leave the nest; the third week they are independent. Immediately, the parents make plans for another family.

Juveniles gather in small flocks. They feed on the ground, picking up seeds and insects and a variety of grains found in fields. Their preference for weed seeds and grasshoppers makes them especially useful to the farmer. They sometimes visit farms and feed with pigeons and farmyard fowl. In six months they are mature, sleek, streamlined, pigeonlike birds.

The gray-blue plumage of the mourning dove, washed with golden overtones, has tints of pink and blue delicately interwoven into the head and neck feathers. The female usually wears dove-gray. Mourning doves are about ten inches long and spread their wings twelve inches. Long, pointed tails with white-tipped side feathers distinguish them from other members of the pigeon and dove family.

In August, the mourning doves gather in large flocks to make sprightly flights on whistling wings, in preparation for the long flight south. Many times they perch on telephone wires and swing in the breeze.

A hard frost in September tells them they can no longer delay. The young birds leave first, followed by great flights of adults. The migrants do not all return to their winter homes; many meet with accidents on the way.

Zenaidura macroura, the mourning dove, is considered a game bird in many areas; in others, he is a songbird and is protected. There are two subspecies in America. Although mourning doves have a reputation for being gentle, peaceful birds, they are very hardy, self-sufficient, and wary. Even the blue jay, bully that he is, cannot intimidate the mourning dove. The hunter has not decreased their sizable numbers.

Willow Ptarmigan

PTARMIGAN country is far to the north in the land of the midnight sun. The Willow Ptarmigan, a small arctic grouse about thirteen inches in length, is well adapted to the rigorous climate in which he lives. Nature provides him with the most wonderful protection—plumage which changes to meet the changing seasons.

In winter when all the world is white, the willow ptarmigan is dressed in a white coat of the softest, warmest down. A tight, well-oiled overcoat protects the body from cold winds and wet snow. The legs and feet are clad in feathered boots; spiny hairlike feathers grow out from the sides of the feet to enable the bird to walk on the soft snow. Toenails become long and sharp. These are used like ice picks for holding to slippery surfaces. A black beak and black tail feathers are carried through all the seasons.

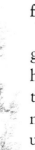

During the most severe weather, the ptarmigan moves to valleys and sheltered coves to feed on tips of willows and alders. Often he is seen along windswept slopes or on the open tundra. When blizzards rage, he flies into snowbanks for warmth and shelter. An airhole through the snow supplies oxygen. Occasionally, though, a bird is imprisoned in an icebound igloo from which he cannot escape.

As the winter nights grow shorter, the loud hooting calls of the mating season begin. Now the ptarmigan flock together, the males to preen, the females to observe and choose a mate. Red-hot tempers flare. Many battles take place in which the strongest contestants win the prize. Each male usually has but one mate. He remains steadfast and true to her, giving protection until the family is raised in late summer.

The nest of the ptarmigan is a simple hollow in the ground, lined with grass, leaves, moss, and feathers. The male keeps a constant vigil while the hen sits on five to ten brown-blotched eggs. He employs the age-old ruse of the broken wing to lure enemies away from the nesting site, but frequently men, the arctic fox, and wolf find it despite his persistant efforts. Gulls rob unattended nests in the coastal regions.

Baby ptarmigan are small, lively creatures. They obey the parent's call of

Willow Ptarmigan
1/2 life size
(17 in.)

alarm that tells them to freeze in their tracks when danger is near. Another note signals them to fly to brushy cover or broken rocks for protection. A soft cluck tells them to reassemble.

The summer plumage of the ptarmigan is reddish brown, with mottled grayish-tan and black markings. This coloring so closely matches the tundra and rocks that the birds are practically invisible when on the ground. The families move southward into central Canada and range into the interior to feed on berries, seeds, insects, and herbs. In autumn a few white feathers appear in the brown plumage as they once more turn northward to their arctic home.

Lagopus lagopus, the willow ptarmigan, is larger and more common than either *Lagopus leucurus,* the white-tailed ptarmigan, or the rock ptarmigan, *Lagopus mutus.* They are all closely related, inhabiting the same range in some areas, and extending farther north and south in others. The white-tail is seen as far south as the Rockies of New Mexico. The rock ptarmigan is an inhabitant of the arctic islands of the North.

Chukar Partridge

THE CHUKAR PARTRIDGE is another game bird that has been successfully introduced in America. It was originally a native of the Middle East and Southern Asia and is particularly adapted to the semiarid slopes and sagebrush lands of the West. These birds do well in southern Canada also.

The chukar gets his name from his clucking *"chuck-chuck-chuc-kar"* call. He is larger than a quail and smaller than a grouse, measuring about ten inches in length. The sexes are similar, although the female is slightly more subtle in coloring. The backs are bluish-gray with a hint of brown in some, with white and buff underparts. Reddish-brown stripes mark the flanks. The chukar may be distinguished from the gray partridge by a black border which begins at the base of the bill, runs back through the eye, down the side of the neck, and forms a "V" on the breast. The black necklace separates a whitish throat from the buffy under-feathers. This bird also has reddish-orange feet and legs with spurlike knobs on the backs, which are somewhat larger in the males. He bears the scientific name of *Alectoris graeca.*

In late winter, the males tend to gather in small flocks in open places in flats or on sunny slopes, and make ready for the mating season which is just ahead. Many bluffing battles take place among them. Pairing begins in March, and nesting activities commence in mid-April and early May. Each male may have one female or several, which he defends from other males.

The female scrapes a depression in the ground, usually on a slope above a stream or some source of water, where it is well concealed by shrubs or clumps of grass. Many times the nest is found at the base of a cliff near a canyon rim, among rocks and brush. It is lined with grass, leaves, twigs, and feathers. Stealthily the female approaches and leaves each time she lays a brownish, spotted egg. Deserted by the male, she sits on her clutch, which varies from nine to twenty eggs, but usually about twelve, for twenty-four days.

Downy chukar chicks are active as soon as they are dry. They follow the mother from the nest to scratch in the dirt and search for insects and seeds. They come when she calls, or hide instantly if she gives a warning, for many predators lie in wait for the partridge family, especially the bobcat and hawk. During the day the birds sun themselves in protected slopes where they lounge and dust themselves. Weeds, grass seeds, tender flower shoots, and leaves, as well as many insects, are devoured. In late summer the partridges forage in oak and juniper groves, visit stubble fields and consume waste grain. Wild fruit and berries are welcome in any season, rich and juicy when ripe, or dried on the bushes in winter.

In the fall, families mingle in large flocks. They find shelter beneath overhanging cliffs or in the underbrush, and when the snow covers their feeding grounds, they move to lower elevations, or fly to higher places on the mountains where they feed on windswept slopes.

The chukar is wary, adept at the art of concealment, and has the odd habit of running uphill when pursued. His flight is direct, strong, and usually low.

Many of our states and Canada have game farms where the birds are raised and released in favorable habitat when they are old enough to survive in the wild state. Where flocks are well managed, they have prospered and the chukar now ranks high as a favorite game bird.

Canada Goose

THE CLARION call of a Canada Goose rings across a southern marsh. Restless flocks hear the welcome summons and take to the air with noisy, slow-flapping wings. Led by trail-wise ganders, they form wedges or line out in single file. Their hoarse honking is swallowed by the wind as they disappear beyond the horizon. Guided by a mysterious homing instinct, the wild Canada "honkers" head north toward their ancestral breeding grounds.

The flights fan out across the northern part of the United States and southern Canada. Some geese stay in the northwestern states, others wing on to breeding grounds in Newfoundland, Labrador, Hudson Bay, and across the tundra to Alaska and western Canada.

Branta canadensis, the Canada goose, is a gray-brown bird, the largest goose in America. There are about ten subspecies, smaller and slightly different in coloring and habits. All are recognized by their long black necks and heads with a white band running around the throat from cheek to cheek. They weigh up to fourteen pounds and have a wingspread of six feet or more.

The Canadas mate for life. Each pair returns in the spring to an old nesting site near the place where they were reared. The nest, made of grass and reeds, and softly padded with down from the mother's breast, is usually found on mounds along the banks of lakes and rivers, or in open tundra near marshes. The mother lays six to ten white eggs. The gander, ill-tempered during the nesting season, guards her.

Downy, yellow goslings take to the water as soon as they are hatched. Father is the leader; mother guards them from the rear. The parents teach the young to forage for water plants, grass, seeds, and some insects. They grow fast under the careful guardianship of their parents.

During late spring, and shortly after the babies have hatched, the adults lose their feathers in a molt. The young have not yet learned to fly, so the family is now earthbound. During this critical period the geese must depend on their swimming ability to evade their enemies. When danger threatens, the parents come to the defense of the young with feathers rustling, wings beating, heads outstretched, and hissing fierce warnings. The young birds hide in the

Canada Goose
1/6 life size
(35-42 in.)

grass or dive beneath the water for protection. At night they roost on the water with their heads tucked beneath their wings. A careful watch is kept for large pike, otter, the fox, and hawks, as well as men.

In mid-August the geese gather in large flocks and take to the air. In their southward flight they pause at the great grainfields of the Midwest to feed on the grain scattered among the stubble after the harvest. During the day they return to the shores of rivers or lakes to rest and gabble in little groups. Sentinels stand guard with black necks high in the air.

The young geese fly south with the parents and return with them to the north in the spring. The southern flight is by far the most dangerous. Hunters wait along the line of flight to kill the great geese as they come to earth to feed and rest. As a result, many of the large flocks reported in early days have been destroyed.

In recent years more and more game refuges have been established to protect the Canada geese in all their ranges. Shooting has been controlled, and young birds have been reintroduced in areas where they had disappeared. Slowly the goose population is rising, and the sight of these great birds will continue to stir the imagination of men as they stand earthbound and observe the wild geese flying free above their heads.

Whistling Swan

MOST people have never seen the wild Whistling Swan. Their breeding grounds are far from civilization in the most isolated regions of the North. From the banks of Hudson Bay across the Barren Grounds of Canada, to the Arctic Sea, and along the northern Alaskan coast, the whistling swans summer. They winter southward from Alaska to the northern part of the United States and are fairly common in the Great Basin. But even in refuges where they are protected, the swans are shy and wary and avoid contact with men.

The whistling swan (*Olor columbianus*) is the most common swan in America. Of all our waterfowl, he ranks second in size only to the very rare trumpeter. An adult weighs about sixteen pounds, averages fifty-two inches in length, and measures almost seven feet across the wings. Whether gliding gracefully on the glassy surface of an icebound lake or flying overhead with translucent wings slowly flapping, the whistling swans are regal birds.

The whistling swan may be told from the trumpeter by a yellow mark above the bill and by its pure white wings in flight. Both have black bills, feet, and legs.

Flying very high and fast, the swans begin their northward journey in the spring, and their loud, high-pitched, quavering voices at this time may have given them their name. They form a V or string out in long, undulating ribbons. Sometimes they are forced to land by heavy winds or sleet storms. Otherwise, they fly directly to their goal, stopping only to rest and eat.

Young swans remain with their parents for the first year. In their second they usually mate before leaving the South. Once they have chosen a mate, swans remain constant for the remainder of their lives.

They nest on the banks of large rivers, marshes, and lakes. The cob, or male, assists with building a large, bulky structure of reeds, leaves, and moss. The pen, as the female is called, does the setting, carefully guarded by her faithful mate. He stretches his long neck high in the air and turns his head like a periscope. When the pen leaves the nest she covers her four to seven eggs with moss to keep them warm and protect them.

By the first of July the fuzzy cygnets, dressed in gray down with pink bills and feet, glide gracefully in open water. The adults feed the young by reaching to the bottom of shallow pools and marshes to obtain water plants, shoots, and bulbs. Along the banks they feed on tender grass. When the young are tired of sailing, they climb on their parents' backs. Here they are safe from storms and their enemies. Some say they are hoisted aboard by stepping on the adult's foot. This may be true, for swans swim in leisurely fashion with one webbed foot, while the other rests by their sides.

During the summer the swans molt, and natives hunt them at this time in boats and afoot. Many fall prey to the hunters, but others escape by running swiftly on land or by evading their pursuers in the reeds.

In October the northern waterways are churned by many paddling feet and beating wings. The swans circle their northern haunts, high quavering voices whistling a last farewell, and under leaden skies, they point their heads south toward their winter homes.

Green-winged Teal

A HUSH of expectancy mantles the marsh. The voice of feeding ducks is stilled. Suddenly and with amazing speed the flock vaults into the air. *"Kuk-kuk-kuk!"* The cry of alarm and the reedy whistle of singing wings floats back to earth. Flying swiftly, the compact mass angles upward, wheels, and levels off at a high altitude. The birds are soon lost to sight. A flash of green on the wings, the white underparts, the short necks, and the small size identify the ducks of this flight as Green-winged Teal.

The green-winged teal (*Anas carolinensis*) is a small, hardy duck. Teal remain in the North until snow and ice cover their feeding grounds, and in some places in the West they remain near open water all year. Others migrate southward to Mexico and the Gulf States and along the eastern seaboard. The spring migration of the teal northward begins early in March, shortly behind the mallard. Their breeding grounds extend from Alaska east to Hudson Bay and south through the Great Plains and the western part of the United States.

The drake is a mottled gray-and-brown dandy with a green spot surrounding the eye, a chestnut head, a dark crest, and a bright green rectangle on the wings which gives him his name. He courts the diminutive female by swimming in circles about her, bobbing his head back and forth and preening his burnished feathers. A love note, *"Pheep-pheep,"* proclaims his affection. The female replies with a low *"Queek."*

The duck conceals her nest in a clump of grass well back from the water. One by one she lays six to twelve olive-buff eggs. When the clutch is complete, she settles down to incubate. Each time she leaves the nest for a short swim and to feed, she carefully covers the eggs with down.

Small, damp ducklings break from the shells. In a few hours they dry into fuzzy balls of down with wide bills and bright eyes. The lively youngsters are curious and eager to go adventuring into the world. The mother, left to rear her children alone, is a devoted and courageous guardian. She protects them from rats and hawks, and teaches them to dabble along muddy banks in search of insects, waterplants, and seeds. The young ducks stand on their heads in shallow water and probe the mud for tender bulbs and sprouts. This

Green-winged Teal
1/2 life size
(13-15½ in.)

is called "tipping." Grass, wild celery, wild rice, oats, and pondweeds are favorite foods. Most ducks waddle about on the land, but the teal are adept at walking and even run swiftly. In the woods they feed on acorns, dry berries, and herbs. Near farms they make morning and evening excursions to feed in grainfields. The young teal are full-fledged in July.

The drakes desert the females when they go to nest, and join other males to spend their time feeding, swimming, and sunning themselves on sandbars and mud-flats. A continuous molt takes them from the brown summer plumage, in which they resemble the females and juveniles, into their winter finery.

There are two other well-known teal in America: the blue-winged teal and the cinnamon teal. Both have pale blue patches on the forward edge of the wings, and the cinnamon teal has a cinnamon-red head and underparts. Both are slightly larger than the green-winged teal.

Wood Duck

THE WOOD DUCK is well named. He is indeed a woodsman. He loves ponds, inland lakes, rivers, and marshes fringed with open woods. Without both water and trees, these beautiful ducks disappear from the landscape.

Go to a wood-duck pond in April if you would see the most colorful of all our native American waterfowl at their best. The small ducks, less than twenty inches in length, sail about on the water or loiter in groups on the banks. Never a quack is heard, but the air is filled with the low whistles and anxious chatter of the mating season. The handsome drake is resplendent in iridescent hues of blue, green, purple, and golden brown. White lines streak from the bill to the end of the long, green crest. Peculiar white patches decorate the cheeks. The drab, brown female has but one mark of distinction—a white teardrop which surrounds the eye, giving her a wide-eyed, startled expression.

A drake and his lady swim side by side, caress, and fly to the woods in search of a nesting place. They prefer a hollow tree, but if such a natural cavity is not to be found, the female may worm her plump body into a woodpecker's hole. This she enlarges to her own liking, and lines it with down from her breast. Here is an excellent hiding place for eight to sixteen white eggs.

The vain drake perches on a branch while his mate works at nest building. He switches his tail, preens his feathers, and whistles soft love notes. But if danger threatens he warns her with a siren call of alarm. Then their flight is swift and direct. They seem to melt through tangled branches and trees. The mother hardly falters as she enters her nest at breakneck speed.

Downy ducklings hatch in twenty-eight days. They are barely two days old when the mother coaxes them from the tree house. The babies use sharp toenails and hooked beaks to scale the inside of the tree trunk. They balance on the threshold for a moment, then bravely flutter to the ground and make their way to the nearest pond or stream. Soon they are launched in the water.

Along the banks of streams and ponds the wood ducks paddle, searching for water plants and seeds. A short walk takes them to the woods where they greedily consume acorns, dry berries, seeds, nuts, insects, and grass. They perch on moss-grown logs which have fallen into the water, and doze in the sun. At night they rest in sheltered inlets, heads tucked beneath their wings.

During the summer the drakes lose their beautiful plumage and grow less spectacular coats of subdued tones. Several families may merge to form larger autumn flocks. Wood ducks are found throughout temperate North America. In winter they migrate southward to the Gulf of Mexico, but in many areas they are seen during every month of the year.

Aix sponsa, the wood duck, has been saved from extinction by protective game laws. Today it thrives in duck refuges across the United States and southern Canada. In some areas it nests in man-made boxes. It is so friendly and trusting that it even graces many private pools.

Red-headed Duck

AYTHYA AMERICANA, the Red-headed Duck, is an exceptionally fine game bird. During the seasons of migration, flocks are commonly seen on inland lakes, rivers, bays, and ponds. During the winter, the redheads frequent marshy tidelands along our coasts and the Gulf of Mexico.

Redheads are often seen in company with the canvasback, a slightly larger duck with a whitish back and longer neck. The two are quite similar in appearance, but can be told apart by the shape of their heads. In the canvasback, a long bill slopes gradually to the top of the head. In the redhead, the forehead rises abruptly from a short blue bill. The redhead has a silvery-gray back etched with wavy, black lines. The males have chestnut-red heads and dark breasts. The females are brownish in color.

Well behind early migrating waterfowl, the redheads leave the tidelands of the South, flying in V-shaped formations. Most of the early arrivals are already mated when they reach their northern breeding grounds in the United States and central and southern Canada. The female takes an active part in the mating display on the water. In the courtship flights, the drake pursues her with reckless abandon, following her zigzag course so closely that he seems to be glued to her tail feathers.

The nest is a sturdy wicker basket structure woven of dry marsh grass, the bottom and sides lined with white down. It sits above the water concealed by tall reeds. Although the female has such a fine nest in which to lay her large clutch of olive-buff eggs, she often drops them in the nests of other ducks. When the female retires to the nest and the sitting begins in earnest, the drake deserts her and leaves her to rear the family alone.

Ten to sixteen lively ducklings require a lot of protection and attention, but the proud little mother is equal to the task. During the first weeks the family dabbles along the banks like common puddle ducks. The babies are expert swimmers and divers, and the mother seems not to be concerned when they disappear beneath the water. In fact, she often quacks to alert them to danger and the little ones dive and swim to safe hiding places in the grass. In deep ponds they feed on minnows, and the tender shoots of water plants.

Red-headed Duck
1/3 life size
(23 in.)

As soon as the adults recover from the spring molt, they gather in large flocks to "raft" in open water and feed. Coots and baldpate ducks often mingle with them and steal the food which they bring to the surface. In return for the handouts, these nervous ducks act as sentinels while the redheads feed. Many times each day the flocks rise from the surface as though frightened, then restlessly settle down to feed again.

Early in the summer mornings, small companies of redheads make training flights, either from sheer love of flying or in preparation for the fall migration. They paddle along the surface of the water for a short distance before taking to the air with much noisy calling. When approaching unfamiliar waters, the flocks carefully survey the territory before landing.

Redheads leave their northern homes well in advance of the freezing weather. They are usually settled in their winter homes while other waterfowl still linger in the North.

Mallard

THE MALLARD is one of our most widely distributed and best-known waterfowl. We cannot claim this duck as solely a native to America; he is found in many other parts of the world as well. Some of our best-known domestic strains of ducks have been developed from the mallard (*Anas platyrhynchos*).

The mallard is a large, hardy duck, handsome, wary, and wise. In America he is found from Alaska to Mexico; from the Pacific to the Atlantic; from the mountains to the lowlands, but is perhaps most common in the northwestern part of the continent. In the spring he is among the first migrants, pushing north in the wake of melting ice and snow. In the fall he lingers until the water is icelocked and all the feeding grounds are snow-covered.

The drake can be identified by the glossy green head, white collar, burnished chest, curling, white-edged tail feathers, and yellow bill. The female is brownish gray, smaller than the drake, with a dark bill. Both have a shiny blue rectangle on the hind edge of the wings, yellow feet and legs, and white underwings seen only in flight. The drake averages two and one-half pounds in weight and has a wingspread of about thirty-four inches.

Early in the spring the drakes display their fine plumage before the quacking females. With much bobbing, bowing, and circling they whistle softly and vie with other males. Several drakes may be seen coursing over the marshes in pursuit of a female. During the courtship chase, the female may touch the body of her chosen mate with her bill; the two then fly away together.

The duck makes her nest in a clump of tall marsh grass, or beneath bushes near the bank of streams and sloughs. Fickle drakes desert the female ducks in the early days of nesting. The males gather in small groups and remain in seclusion during the summer molt.

Left to rear her family alone, the mother carefully incubates the clutch of greenish-buff eggs. Before leaving the nest for short periods, she covers them with down and leaves or grass to keep them warm and to conceal them from thieving crows and other predators.

Mother Mallard has been seen with eight to sixteen ducklings, which can swim when they are a few hours old. The mother duck boldly chases muskrats and small enemies from the vicinity. She decoys men and larger predators away from her young. The babies can run fast, swim swiftly, and are obedient to every command. The mother has many notes which she uses as signals. There is a feeding call, an alarm, and a "come-hither" call. Without any training, the ducklings dive beneath the water and swim to shelter in the marshes. In six weeks they can fly.

Late in August the drakes, having molted their wing feathers, appear in their "eclipse" plumage. At this time they resemble the juveniles and females. There is much noisy chatter on the feeding grounds. In the marshes the ducks strip seeds from waterplants or feed on tender shoots and stems. They seldom dive for food, but with a "tip" of their tails and flailing feet above the surface they probe in the shallows with their wide bills. Acorns, hazelnuts, and other vegetation form a part of their diet. Mosquito larvae, mussels, tadpoles, and small fish are also eaten. Their food supply is as varied as their habitat.

Many of the large flocks of mallards which were formerly seen have disappeared, yet despite hunting and destruction of their nesting sites, they are still quite prevalent. Game refuges shelter many, and private individuals are lending a hand to assist in reclaiming marshy land for their benefit.

Belted Kingfisher

NO MATTER what time of day a fisherman goes to his favorite fishing hole, there may be another there before him. The Belted Kingfisher is the large blue-gray bird so often seen flying along streams, rivers, and ponds. Suddenly he falters as his keen eyes see a fish below, then power-dives toward the water. He disappears beneath the surface and emerges with a wriggling fish in his bill. Off he flies triumphant to a nearby perch, and swallows his catch head first. Once heard, his rattling call is never forgotten.

Dressed in an eye-catching coat of blue with a white collar, a blue band emblazoned across his chest and a rather ragged crest, Mr. Kingfisher is a handsome bird. If anything, Mrs. Kingfisher is even more picturesque than her husband, with an extra band of rufous brown across her breast. These king-fishers are solitary birds, usually seen alone or in pairs. Few fishing holes can support a whole flock.

The long, straight, strong bill of the kingfisher makes a fine fishing spear. It is also used as a digging tool. In May a pair of kingfishers choose a spot on a steep, sandy bank to build a nest; not one of grass and feathers, but a long tunnel dug into the earth. With their bills they loosen the dirt. With their short legs and small feet they remove it from the burrow. Working in shifts, they can dig five feet in two days. Although last year's burrow may be only a few feet away, the hardworking kingfishers allow the swallows to occupy it, while they dig a new one for themselves.

In a dark chamber at the end of an incline, the mother lays one white egg each day until there are six or eight. For seventeen days the pair take turns warming them. While one sits, the other patrols a mile of stream they claim as their territory. Trespassers are warned away with loud scolding calls.

The newly hatched babies are completely nude. Their eyes are closed. They have large heads, mouths, stomachs, and appetites. The parents must fish long hours to feed their charges. The young birds open their eyes in ten days, and by the seventeenth they are much larger. Pinfeathers protrude in sharp points from their bodies. On the eighteenth day, a miracle! The pinfeathers burst and blossom into full plumage, exactly like that of the adults except for

56

Belted Kingfisher
3/4 life size
(11-14 in.)

a brownish tinge on the chests. In four weeks they leave the dugout.

The parents' responsibility does not end yet. They must teach the young birds to search along the streams with their sharp eyes alert for prey. They learn the art of hovering and diving. Kingfishers can spot a fish from fifty feet in the air. Sometimes they bring to the surface chubs that prey on eggs and young of game fish, or frogs, tadpoles, water insects, mollusks, and other water creatures. When fishing is poor, they find berries and insects in the woods. Many times their bills are empty. It takes a lot of practice to become a good fisherman.

The sturdy, patient kingfisher belongs to a worldwide family. Only two kinds are known in this country, the small green kingfisher of the Southwest, and the more common belted kingfisher (*Megaceryle alcyon*). Larger than a robin—about twelve inches in length—this well-known species breeds from Alaska to Mexico. They winter wherever they find open water. The kingfisher is rightly named king of the fishermen.

Common Loon

WHEN this continent was first settled, almost every small pond or large lake from the arctic islands to the northern part of the United States was a summer home for nesting Common Loons. Many of those watering places are empty now, but across an occasional lonely lake an eerie, wild, laughing cry still warns intruders to keep away. This is the private property of the loon.

The handsome loon is dressed in tight, compact feathers and thick down. The breeding plumage is a striking pattern of intricate black and white checks, stripes, and polka dots. The large head and moderately long neck are as smooth as black velvet, with greenish highlights.

The solitary, unsociable loons build their nests on the shores of deep, clear lakes, marshy bays, riverbanks, or sometimes on a muskrat house in a quiet lagoon. Though highly specialized divers and graceful swimmers, on land loons lumber about on short legs placed so far to the rear of their bodies that they cannot walk upright. They flounder about, pushing with their feet and scooting on their breasts, as they push a mass of vegetation together at the very edge of the water. Here the female lays two large, olive-green eggs. For almost a month the pair take turns sitting. To keep the eggs warm, they tuck them against a bare brood patch between the legs.

Baby loons are covered with soft, sooty-brown down. A few days after hatching, the little ones hop into the water behind the parents, and here they remain until they can fly. The small ones take many water excursions on the mother's back.

Water is a haven for the loons. Here they find protection from their enemies and fish for food. They swim low in the water as though ready to submerge at the slightest hint of danger, and they disappear so unobtrusively that they hardly leave a ripple. They can swim underwater by holding the bill above the surface. They are unexcelled as divers, plunging as much as 170 feet in pursuit of fish, and they execute fantastic underwater maneuvers by using the broad webbed feet for propellers and the wings for extra spurts of speed. The stout, evenly tapered bills are as deadly as daggers. They eat fish morning, noon, and night, and in addition feed on crabs, crayfish, shellfish, aquatic insects, and vegetation. After the nesting season the adults separate and molt their winter feathers.

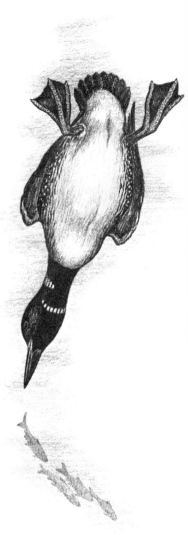

When ice begins to seal the northern waters, loons migrate south. They labor into the air by running along the surface of the water, their narrow, pointed wings beating furiously. Finally, with the aid of a head wind, they are aloft. They fly singly or in pairs. Rarely are more than four or five seen in a group. The heads are held lower than the bodies and the legs trail out behind the short, stiff tails. Most of them winter along the Atlantic and Pacific coasts and the Gulf of Mexico. Some go to open inland lakes.

Loons are among our most primitive birds. They are larger than ducks and smaller than geese, and measure up to thirty-four inches in length with a wingspread of fifty-eight inches.

Four species of loons inhabit the American continent; the yellow-billed loon, the red-throated loon, the arctic loon. and the common loon. The common loon (*Gavia immer*) is the most widely distributed.

Arctic Tern

MIGRATION champion of the world is the Arctic Tern, a beautiful, stream-lined sea-bird which makes a round trip of 22,000 miles each year between its summer and winter ranges. He belongs to a large family of which there are thirty-nine species scattered around the world. Some of them look so much alike that only experts can positively identify them. The sexes are similar, and to add confusion, winter adults and juveniles are almost identical.

Sterna paradisaea, the light-hearted arctic tern, is a gray-mantled bird with long, narrow wings, short legs, webbed feet, black-capped head, and a slender, blood-red bill. A long, forked swallowtail has given him the name of sea swallow.

In the spring when arctic ice masses are breaking up, thousands of terns descend in gray clouds on the shores of northernmost islands and along the coasts of Alaska, Canada, Labrador, and south to New England. In their breeding grounds they nest in teeming colonies, occasionally in company with common terns and gulls.

The courtship of the tern begins when a male ceremoniously presents a female with a small fish, probably as an engagement gift. The female accepts the offering and zooms into the air. A headlong chase follows. The fish is passed from bill to bill as the birds execute swift flying maneuvers, their powerful wings carrying them in steep upward spirals and gliding descents. High-pitched screams of *"Kee-kee, kee-ar-r"* are heard throughout the flight.

The nest of the tern is a "scrape" in the sand—a small depression made as the female pirouettes on her breast and pushes the sand about with her feet. The two brownish-tan or green eggs with reddish-brown spots she lays look like stones amid the rubble on the beach. Some terns adorn their nests with seashells and bright pebbles. Tundra nests are sparsely lined with dry grass.

For three precious weeks the male and female take turns warming the eggs during days of almost continuous daylight. The babies are brooded for several days in the nest, then left alone while the parents search for food. Crabs, herring gulls, weasels, foxes, and skunks prey on the eggs and the young birds.

Arctic Tern
1/2 life size
(14-17 in.)

Terns fly with their slender bills pointed downward and their heads moving from side to side as their eyes scan the water for schools of fish. Although they are not considered swimming birds, they will dive head first into the water after their prey. Crustacea, insects, and fish are crammed into the throats of waiting babies. After two weeks the parents drop feed from the air and the fledglings serve themselves; in a month they can fly.

Summer ends. The days grow short. The terns now desert their breeding grounds and go to the oceans. For the juveniles, this is the first trip to the winter homes in the southern hemisphere; for many of the older birds it may be the tenth or eighteenth trip; for all it is the longest migratory journey made by any bird. Terns that nested in the east fly to the French coast and down the Atlantic along western Africa. Others fly down the Pacific Coast. In some unknown way they make their way across vast oceans to the antarctic islands, a journey of more than 10,000 miles. In this long flight the arctic terns seem to be following the sun. From the arctic summer in the land of the midnight sun, they fly to the antarctic summer where again the sun never sets during their stay.

Herring Gull

ALONG the seacoasts, inland lakes, and rivers of our land the raucous voices of sea gulls fill the air as they swoop and whirl in wonderful sailing flights above the water. There are at least twenty species of gulls in America, but the best known is the beautiful, gray-mantled Herring Gull, a large bird about twenty-four inches long.

The herring gull is called *Larus argentatus* by scientists. Other people frequently refer to him as the harbor gull. These gulls show little fear of men. They are at home in harbors, rivers, and waterways near large cities. As scavengers they are among our most beneficial birds, feeding on dead fish and waste which empties into the ocean and rivers from sewage systems. They follow fishing vessels, quarreling over bits of waste thrown overboard.

The plumage of both sexes is the same, so it is difficult to tell them apart. Brown individuals may be seen mingling with the white birds in a flock. These are juveniles in their first and second years. By their third or fourth year, the young have attained the beautiful pearl-gray mantle, black-tipped wings, pink feet, and yellow bills with a red spot on the underside which mark the adult.

Gulls are highly social birds. They feed in large flocks and nest in colonies near water. Their moss- and grass-lined nests are found on the ground, on cliffs, on rocky ledges, and in tall trees.

The love note of the gull is a buglelike blare, quite different from the feeding call or the cry of alarm. Males display themselves and parade before indifferent females on sandbars and sandy beaches. A characteristic chase through the sky seals the betrothal. Three or four bluish-green eggs, spotted and lined with brown, are incubated by both adults. For a week after hatching, the babies are brooded in the nest to protect them from sun, rain, and predators, including older gulls which often kill the young birds.

The young birds are fed by regurgitation of partly digested food. They soon learn to raise their bills when adults approach the nest and beg for their dinner. In five weeks they have their flight feathers and mingle in flocks with other brown juveniles.

Herring gulls are mostly scavengers. They comb the beaches looking for dead fish and other refuse, sea urchins, clams, mussels, snails, and crabs. Hard-shelled creatures are carried into the air and dropped on hard pavement or rocks to shatter them. The gulls then descend to feed on the contents. They fly over the water and search for schools of fish; when they sight one, they swoop gracefully down, wings flapping, tails spread and feet dangling, to seize their prey with their long beaks. They seldom dive but are extremely good swimmers, using their webbed feet to good advantage.

After the breeding season, which they usually spend along the coasts of Canada or the North Atlantic states, some herring gulls become wanderers and travel far and wide. Early in the mornings large flocks fly out to sea. Some travel inland to freshwater lakes and rivers. In winter they move south, sometimes as far as Mexico. They feed in plowed fields and in stubble patches. Some of these gulls roost in trees at night; others on rocky shores. When they are molested, they fly to open water and ride the waves. They are protected in most areas, and have learned to approach picnickers and beg for a share of their lunch, or to settle on the prow of a ship without fear.

Great Blue Heron

THE GREAT BLUE HERON is a picturesque, aristocratic, long-legged wading bird. *Ardea herodias* is the common Latin name by which he is known. Many people call him the Blue Crane. But although he bears some resemblance to this family, he is not a crane, for cranes fly with necks outstretched like geese. The great blue heron flies with his long neck looped and the slender, black-crested head resting almost on the shoulders. In flight, long legs trail straight behind the short tail. Powerful wings beat slowly, steadily, almost rhythmically. When standing on his stiltlike legs, the heron reaches a height of four feet, although he weighs something less than eight pounds.

The great blue heron is a marvelous fisherman. Patiently the solemn bird stands perfectly motionless in shallow water, surrounded by tall marsh grass. He also feeds in open water, fully exposed to view. Large, staring eyes, set low and to the front of the head, watch for fish, frogs, eels, salamanders, and water insects. The strong, yellow bill is held in readiness. Suddenly, quicker than the wink of an eye, the neck streaks out and the dagger-bill does its work. The squirming prey is quickly dashed to death and swallowed whole. Once more the bird resumes his stately stance. A slow, high-stepping stroll through the shallows is another profitable method of fishing.

Lone hunters through late summer, fall, and early winter, great blue herons return each year to old rookeries to mate and raise their families. They nest in colonies; often several pairs close together in the tops of tall trees of mangrove swamps and swampy, wooded waterways. In some marshy areas, the nest is built on a platform of rushes above the shallow water. Wary and suspicious, the herons frequent secluded spots.

A wide platform of jumbled sticks, carelessly thrown together but with a soft lining of dry grass, cradles from three to six blue-green eggs. Most young birds which come from the egg already clothed in down are ready to run about and search for their food in a few hours. Baby herons are covered with down when hatched, but are dependent on their parents for several weeks. The grotesque, scrawny, hungry-looking creatures sit on their slim haunches or hop about on their platform. The rookeries are odorous and

Great Blue Heron
1/5 life size
(42-52 in.)

filled with commotion as parents alternately flap away and return to the nests to feed their young on predigested food. There is much squawking, grunting, and croaking.

Gray pinfeathered bodies slowly acquire flight feathers. Young birds have no crests, but stiff hairlike feathers stand up on top of the heads, which with the long bills and staring eyes gives them a fierce appearance. They do a lot of limbwalking before they learn to fly.

The families separate after the nesting season and solitary herons visit far places. Hardly a water area in America but sees at least one great blue heron each year, for their range covers most of the continent. Kelp beds, salt marshes, ponds, inland lakes, rivers, hills, wet pastures, and irrigated fields attract them.

Fish is a favorite delicacy, but they also consume numerous mice, gophers, moles, grasshoppers, and other harmful insects, which should compensate for the few game fish taken. When northern ponds and waters freeze, the great blue heron moves south. Some return to southern refuges; some go to salt marshes near the oceans; others migrate to Mexico and South America.

Great blue herons are commonly seen in many areas, but due to their large size and distinctive slate-blue coloring, they are frequently killed by hunters.

American Bittern

SHY, ILLUSIVE, extremely adept at self-concealment, the Bittern is more often heard than seen. *"Choonk-a-lunk, choonk-a-lunk, choonk-a-lunk."* The three-syllable, hollow, pumping call pulses across the marshes and gives the bird several interesting names, such as Thunder Pumper, Dunk-a-doo, and perhaps the most common of all, Stake Driver. His peculiar voice is heard most often during spring and early summer, early in the morning and late in the evening, and may be the only indication that a bittern is making his home nearby. Bitterns are lonely birds, avoiding contact with men and remaining aloof from their own kind, except for a few weeks during the breeding season.

Nature has provided the bittern with wonderful protective plumage of mottled buff and brown. You may search for the bittern in vain, for the skulking bird lies close to the ground and moves swiftly to escape from danger. Among reeds and cattails, he plants his green legs firmly in the ground, lifts his long bill skyward, and compresses his feathers, so that the brown-and-white striped vest becomes a part of the vegetation. One may approach very near before the bittern will fly. With a *"Kok-kok-kok,"* his cry of alarm, he flies low over the rushes and cattails with legs trailing and the black-tipped wings beating fast. From beak to tail he measures up to thirty-four inches.

Beneath brown shoulder feathers the male has white feathers concealed which are raised in ruffs about the upper neck during the mating dance. They ruffle in anger whenever another male approaches his chosen territory and he is called upon to protect his property.

In remote areas, the mother bittern builds her own nest of dry grass stalks. It is a platform about twelve inches in diameter, usually over shallow water. Sometimes it is on the bank of an islet surrounded and protected by tall grass.

Four or five brownish-buff or olive-buff glossy eggs are her special charges for twenty-eight days and she is watchful and fearless in protecting them. But both eggs and newly hatched babies may fall prey to muskrats, mink, snakes, hawks, and owls, despite her best efforts.

Baby bitterns are ugly little snakelike creatures, hungry as only young birds can be. They crowd the edge of the nest and wait for the mother to bring their dinner. As she approaches, each baby in turn grasps her bill in its own and demands food. They are fed by regurgitation. Each day the mother makes many trips to bring fish, frogs, tadpoles, insects, shellfish, mice, or slugs to satisfy the young ones' appetites.

Bitterns are more active during the twilight hours than during the day. As evening falls, they fly from one part of the marsh to another in search of richer feeding areas. They are skillful stalkers, patient and deadly hunters, standing perfectly still from time to time, waiting for prey to come to them.

The American bittern (*Botaurus lentiginosus*) is more common in America than many suppose. They breed from central Canada south to Mexico, and migrate south to the Gulf states and to South America in the winter. In some areas they are year-round residents. It is quite probable that we will have the bittern with us until the last swamp is drained.

White Pelican

PELICANS are large, spectacular birds with moderately long necks, short legs, webbed feet, short tails, and broad, rounded wings which measure eight to ten feet from tip to tip. This is the bird everyone can identify by the extremely large, long bill with a deep pouch hanging below which he uses to scoop up fish. Another unusual feature of the pelican is that all four toes are fastened together by a web—for which pelicans are called *totipalmate swimmers.*

Two pelicans common to America are the Brown Pelican (*Pelecanus occidentalus*), a coastal bird which specializes in high-flying dives; and the White Pelican (*P. erythrorhynchos*) a more widely distributed, western pelican which inhabits both coastal and inland waters.

In April hundreds of white pelicans leave their winter homes in the Gulf of Mexico, southern California, and lower Pacific waters to fly to isolated islands in large inland lakes or marshy waterways. Their breeding grounds extend from northern California east through the Great Basin to the central plains and north to central Canada.

Awkward and ungainly on land, pelicans are transformed into strong, masterful fliers in the air. On migratory journeys they fly in "V" formation, large flocks forming long lines with black-tipped wings alternately flapping and sailing, all in unison. On short flights they form close flocks and fly in smaller numbers.

Pelican rookeries are filled with noisy activity from the time the pelicans arrive until they leave in the fall. Great throngs crowd the islands and banks, grunting and vying for a nesting spot. Nests are usually shallow depressions in the earth, ringed with sticks and debris. Two large, white eggs with rough shells must be incubated for four weeks before they hatch.

Baby pelicans are certainly the ugly ducklings of the bird world. Naked when hatched, the reddish bodies are soon covered with white down. Short bills lengthen and grow wide and thick.

Young pelicans huddle together like frightened sheep when in danger. During the day they stretch their wings to the sun, yawn, or solemnly stand with their grayish bills straight down, resting on the slightly curved necks.

White Pelican
1/7 life size
(55-70 in.)

Just out of the nest, they totter about using the stiff wings for support. Sitting pelicans, newly hatched chicks, and half-grown juveniles may be seen in the same area.

Pelicans, highly social at all times, have learned to fish in companies. Long lines form offshore, wing to wing. Swimming slowly, they drive schools of fish into shallow water where they are scooped up in the pelican's dipnet pouch. When the pouch is empty it can be contracted against the bill.

Babies feed on predigested liquid from the bill of a parent. Older birds thrust their bills, heads, and necks into the open mouths of the adults, reaching down into the gullet or pouch to get fish held there. Frogs, salamanders, and other forms of water life are also consumed.

For a few weeks in the fall, pelicans visit the seacoasts and lakes, ponds, and rivers before turning south. Summer and winter refuges have been established to protect the pelican, for owing to the reduction of their breeding grounds, they are in danger of becoming extinct.

Snowy Egret

MOTIONLESS as an alabaster statue on polished ebony legs, the Snowy Egret poses against a background of swampy vegetation. Immaculate white feathers, narrow, evenly tapered bill, and yellow, jeweled eyes glisten in the sun. Upon this slender beauty scientists have bestowed the name of *Leucophoyx thula;* yellow feet give him the fanciful name of Golden Slippers.

The snowy egret is a small egret of the heron family and one of the most beautiful. He measures twenty-three or twenty-four inches in length, with a wingspread of thirty-four inches. He is a lively feeder, running helter-skelter in pursuit of insects. Although he often stands motionless waiting for a frog or fish, he frequently resorts to stirring or scraping the bottom of shallows with one foot while he stands on the other. Hiding prey are thus exposed to the rapier thrust of the black bill. Fish too large to be swallowed are beaten to a pulpy mass on a rock or tree root before they are consumed.

The male egret in his spring bridal plumage is the most elegant of birds. Delicate feathers crest the head. Long, lacy plumes sprout from the base of the neck and fall across the back like a shimmering veil of spun glass. These exquisite feathers were much in demand at the close of the last century for trimming ladies' hats. Milliners paid a fabulous price of $32.00 an ounce for the "aigrettes"—more than was paid for an ounce of gold. Hunters slaughtered whole colonies of birds for a handful of plumes, which were at their best during the breeding season. Unhatched eggs were left in the nests unattended and young birds died of starvation. Finally protective laws were enacted to save the snowy egret from extinction, but his range is now greatly restricted.

Edward Avery McIlhenny, of Avery Island, Louisiana, must be given much credit for saving the snowy egret. He observed that the egret had all but disappeared from his marshes. Eight fledglings were caged, raised to maturity, and released. The egrets flew away and Mr. McIlhenny waited anxiously for spring. At nesting time they returned, bringing other snowies to share the man-made sanctuary. The colony increased until it now consists of more than 100,000 birds—a wonderful, living monument to the man. There are now also sizeable colonies in the intermountain West.

At the beginning of the mating season the male egret stakes a territory and boastfully proclaims his intent to protect it. Birds of both sexes who venture into his domain are promptly dispatched. A female may return again and again before she is accepted. Then begins a period of billing, caressing, and bold nuptial display. Hoarse croaks and hisses are heard from the usually silent birds.

Together they build a rough platform of sticks in a mangrove tree, in swamp willows, or on matted marsh vegetation above the water. The rickety structure is lined with grass and feathers. Three to six hen-sized eggs of pale blue-green are incubated by both male and female. They are devoted parents; even after the babies are half-grown one stands guard over them most of the time. Babies are fed on thick liquid from the bills of the parents. Later, half-digested fish, frogs, crayfish, shrimps, and insects become their fare. Before they leave the nest on the fourth week, the fledglings have become feathered branch-walkers, using bills as well as long toes to keep their balance.

After the nesting season, snowy egrets wander north and to less populous localities across the United States. They winter in Florida, the Gulf states, southern California, and the coast of Mexico.

Brown Thrasher

THE BROWN THRASHER tells the coming of spring with a sprightly song as musical and mellow as the notes of a piccolo. Nor does he sing for his mate alone; his song is meant for all the world to hear. He flutters up through a tangle of brush to a high perch at the top of a tree, from which he can view the countryside. There he pours his heart out in song. As the tempo of the aria increases, the songster droops his tail, fluffs out his feathers, raises his head, and opens wide his mouth. Rich, melodic notes and intricate phrases, often repeated, bubble forth. For pure musical qualities, only the song of the mockingbird can surpass that of the brown thrasher.

The voice of the brown thrasher (*Toxostoma rufum*) is most commonly heard east of the Rockies where it breeds from southern Canada to the eastern seaboard and south to the Gulf of Mexico. In some areas it is confused with the short-tailed wood thrush. The thrasher can be recognized by his rufous coat with brown stripes on a buffy-white vest, long tail, medium-long bill, curved at the end, and black-and-white-barred wings. He is a slim bird and longer than a robin, measuring ten to twelve inches.

On a cup of a nest made of twigs and lined with rootlets, grass, bark, and a few feathers, the mother thrasher sits tight. Her pale rufous body is well concealed in thorny bushes, on the branch of a low tree, in a pile of brush, or even on the ground in tall vegetation where the nest is hidden. Only her tail extends above the nest as she warms three to six blue-green eggs. Father boldly sings his morning and evening song and heroically defends his family of gawky babies from any danger that threatens. Men, cats, snakes, crows, and other predators are driven away from the nesting site by the brave little warrior. Often the parents join forces and use dive-bombing attacks to frighten intruders.

Naked babies lift their heads on scrawny necks and open their mouths so wide the parents can reach into their throats to deposit grasshoppers, beetles, and other insects, as well as spiders. Although the parents work from dawn till dusk, there never seems to be enough food to supply the hungry youngsters. In little over a week the babies are transformed into bright-eyed birds with a

Brown Thrasher
3/4 life size
(10½ -12 in.)

sparse covering of gray-brown feathers. The parents feed and protect them until they fly and can search for their own food. In the empty nest, the mother lays more eggs and the pair raise another family.

During the spring months the thrasher's diet consists of insects and seeds. Wild fruits and berries ripen in the woods and the farmer's garden in mid-summer and the thrasher turns to them. But for every kernel of grain or berry taken, the thrasher consumes innumerable harmful insects. A lively hunter, he hops and runs about on the ground, twitching his long brown tail from side to side as he feeds.

After the nesting season, the brown thrasher molts into a more uniform fall and winter plumage of buffish-brown and gray. Liquid notes that thrilled the listener in spring are heard no more; the beautiful song is stilled. The thrasher leaves his most northerly summer grounds and returns to the milder climate of the Southeast, where some birds are residents throughout the year.

Mockingbird

THE MOCKINGBIRD is the most accomplished musician of all our American songbirds. He is the master of incomparable medleys and moonlight serenades. His own song is executed with force and eloquence. But he also borrows the songs of other birds, adds his own flourishes, and repeats them over and over. He not only mimics the songs of other birds, but also the sound of an ungreased windmill, the buzz of a saw, or a policeman's whistle. He teases the barnyard fowl by imitating the feeding call of a hen, or the rooster's crow. No wonder scientists have given this bird the realistic Latin name of *Mimus polyglottos,* meaning "mimic of many tongues." The Indians named him "the bird of four hundred tongues." Bird lovers call him the American Nightingale.

The mockingbird delivers his most heart-stirring musicals during the mating season when the male serenades his mate. On moonlight nights he sings on the wing, pouring melodic, liquid notes into the ears of his beloved. He sings as well from a television antenna, the steeple of a village church, a tree in a park, a lawn hedge, or a niche in a porch. The feathers of the slender, gray body and the white underparts tremble with ecstasy and exertion during the prolonged, rollicking song. He raises his wings slightly to show white wing patches, and finally flutters to the ground to rest.

The male carries most of the building materials to the nesting site amid the dense foliage of bushes or the branch of a tree. The female has a way with twigs. She binds them into a sturdy, round cup which she lines with fine

strips of bark, grass, rootlets, and cotton, and feathers to make it soft. Here she lays three to six blue-green eggs which are delicately touched with brown dots. Both parents incubate. It takes from twelve to fourteen days for baby mockingbirds to hatch; then the devoted parents carry so many insects to them that they are ready to leave the nest in ten or twelve days. Young mockingbirds with their brown-streaked breasts resemble their near kinsman, the brown thrasher. When mature, the mockingbird is about ten inches long.

The fledglings soon learn to capture spiders, cotton weevils, beetles, cotton worms, and chinch bugs with their long, curved bills. Their long tails flick nervously from side to side as they hop about on lawns and in gardens. During the summer, mockingbirds feed on fruits and berries. When wild fruit is scarce they inflict some damage on citrus groves, grape vineyards, and cultivated berries.

The mockingbird fiercely defends his territory and family from trespassers, and shows a special dislike for snakes. Quarrelsome and pugnacious, he frequently engages in free-for-all battles with birds of his own kind and even boxes with his image reflected in a window or other shiny surface.

Most people associate the mockingbird with the Deep South and fragrant magnolia blossoms. Actually, he ranges across the entire southern part of the continent from New Jersey to Oregon, and south to Mexico. A western species inhabits the arid desert land of the Southwest and nests in cactus groves and mesquite bushes. In recent years his range has extended to southern Canada. Although the mockingbird is considered nonmigratory, northern birds probably move south with the coming of winter. The states of Arkansas, Florida, Mississippi, Tennessee, and Texas have adopted the mockingbird as their state bird.

Cardinal

WHOIT, *whoit, whoit. Cheer-cheer-cheer. What-cheer, what-cheer."* A series of merry whistled notes pipes across the greening fields at dawn. *"Wake-up wake-up, wake-up,"* the saucy Cardinal seems to say, as he gaily sings from a perch in the top of a tree or shrub.

No one could mistake the proud and beautiful cardinal; he is the only crested red bird in America. From his perky topknot to the tip of the long, slender tail he is dressed in cardinal red, the color for which he is named. Even his feet, legs, and bill are red. A roguish mask of black covers the eyes, upper beak, and chin, contrasting sharply with the firey plumage. In many areas the cardinal is called the Redbird.

The song of the cardinal is one of the few bird songs which is heard throughout the year. In the spring the voice of the male is vibrant and compelling as he sings to his mate. The female is smaller than the male, measuring about seven and one-half inches in length. Although her plumage is much subdued she is still very pretty, with a tinge of red on her wings, tail, and crest, and a pinkish wash on her underparts. Like other members of the finch family, the female cardinal has a rare gift of song. Her soft, melodious warble is thought by some to be even more striking than that of the male.

With a musical flourish, the male marks the boundary of his territory. With a flurry of wings and a sharp call of anger, he quickly drives rivals and intruders from his realm. When all is well, he sings once more.

The female builds a loose nest in thick-flowering shrubs, hedgerows, brush, or thickets. Occasionally she chooses a low tree. The male flits about in the brush like a dancing flame and encourages her in her work. Now and then he brings a twig, a strip of bark, or a bit of soft grass for a lining. He sings while she sits on three or four whitish-blue eggs sprinkled with violet or brown dots. For twelve days he devotedly carries grubs and seeds to her. Willingly he helps her feed the baby cardinals. When the dull brown fledglings leave the nest, it is the father that assumes full responsibility for their future care, while mother cardinal lays more eggs and sits again. During the summer molt the young birds change their brownish coats for plumage

Cardinal
5/6 life size
(8¾ in.)

in which they resemble their parents. In two and one-half months they are independent, and have mastered the cardinal's song.

Cardinals use their short, stout bills to husk sunflower, weed, and wild fruit seeds. Millet, rice, grains, grubs, locusts, grasshoppers, and other harmful insects are added to their menu. In all, they are probably very beneficial to farmers and gardeners.

After the mating season, the cardinals form small flocks and wander about the countryside, but they do not truly migrate. Even the rigorous winters of the North cannot drive them away.

For many years, *Richmondena cardinalis* was numerous in the South but was seldom seen north of Virginia. Growing populations have now pushed north and west, and today, five slightly different subspecies of cardinals are found throughout most of the United States and southern Canada. Seven states have named the cardinal their state bird. Everywhere they are protected, from the Everglades of Florida to the evergreen forests of the North and in the arid desertlands of the Southwest. The cardinal is a loyal citizen in every locality.

Cedar Waxwing

SUMMER fruit and berries are beginning to ripen. The homes of many spring nesters are already cold and deserted. Now flocks of Cedar Waxwings break up, and two by two, the tardy nesters go in search of suitable homesites. The crotch of a sweet cherry tree, a mulberry, or any spot in an orchard, near a berry patch, garden, or in open woods where wild fruit is abundant may be used. Often their nests are found in junipers, cedars, and alder.

It is a shoddy nest they build, this genteel pair of waxwings; quite untidy and makeshift in appearance. Twigs, moss, twine, grass, and a variety of other building materials are used at random. Yet it is sturdy enough to hold from three to six (but usually four), bluish-gray, speckled eggs.

Cedar waxwings are devoted, friendly birds. The male is especially gentle and considerate of his mate. As an engagement present he plucks a flower petal, hops along a branch, and presents it to her. She takes it, but passes it back to him—and so the charming ritual goes. Billing, caressing, and the passing of whispered love notes are all part of the courtship.

Devoted parents carry hundreds of cankerworms, caterpillars, and other insects to their babies. The adults are so trusting that they continue to incubate and care for their young even if they have been touched by human hands. In sixteen days, plump little fledglings, dressed in soft gray, with mottled breasts, are prepared to leave the nest. Soon they develop an appetite for juicy fruit and berries. In no time at all they are independent.

Cedar waxwings are sleek, handsome, well-groomed birds; not a single feather of their soft plumage is ruffled or out of place. A black wedge-shaped patch extends from behind the eye and across the dark bill, with a pointed crest above. The entire dress is one of delicate blending of browns, fawn, gray, and yellow. A bright yellow band tips the dark tail. Curiously, some cedar waxwings have glossy red spots on the upper wings. These spots resemble drops of red sealing wax. From this, and the fact that they frequent cedar forests, they have acquired the common name of cedar waxwing. The scientific name is *Bombycilla cedrorum*. The adult bird is six to eight inches long.

After the nesting season, the cedar birds form small, compact flocks again. In undulating flight, they move from one promising feeding spot to another. They settle deep into the foliage of trees and bushes, gorge themselves until the food has disappeared, or until they cannot hold another bite. Occasionally they line up, all facing in the same direction, and pass a ripe cherry, caterpillar, or other juicy morsel from bill to bill. Each seems too polite to eat it, and so it is passed up and down the line. The mild little birds seldom quarrel or bicker, or even voice their opinions aloud. Although classified as singing birds, they are not songsters in the usual sense. A soft, lisping, beady note is all that is heard as they congregate at their feeding places.

Cedar waxwings do not conform to the usual pattern of north-south migration, although flocks do move around from place to place. Their presence seems to depend upon the availability of food, especially in the winter, when they are often found in the intermountain West as well as some northern states. Southern California, the south central and Gulf states, and Mexico and Panama all have large winter populations.

Meadowlark

THE MEADOWLARK perches on a fencepost to make an important announcement. *"Tee-you, tee-yair. Tee-you, tee-yair."* A loud, bubbling refrain bursts from his throat to tell the farmer, *"Spring is here, spring is here."*

"Old field lark" this gay minstrel is often called, because he loves open fields and meadows. But he is not a lark at all. Like the oriole and blackbird, the meadowlark belongs to the family *Icteridae*. *Sturnella magna* is the meadowlark of the eastern United States. *Sturnella neglecta,* a smaller bird with paler plumage and a vibrant, rollicking song, inhabits the prairies, fields, and upland meadows of the West. Almost every farmer in the United States, southern Canada, and Mexico is familiar with the meadowlark.

Slightly larger than a robin, the meadowlark is a brown bird with darker streaks on the back, and a black crescent emblazoned across the yellow breast. Males arrive in the north two weeks ahead of the females, and proceed to stake out a territory, sometimes as much as seven acres. With their loud, musical songs, they warn all rivals away. When the migrating females arrive, the meadows are filled with excitement as the tempo of the songs increases and opponents battle on the ground for mates. White-edged tail feathers are plainly seen as the birds spiral upward, and then on fast-flapping wings, alternately soaring and beating, return to earth.

The female weaves her nest of grass in a depression in an open field. Sometimes she chooses a spot in a clump of grass near a stream where she goes to bathe. A canopy of interlaced grass covers four to seven white eggs spotted with reddish-brown. If there is enough building material at hand, she constructs a covered walkway with a secret entrance. The structure is artfully concealed from the searching eyes of the hawk, owl, and cat. Of all the enemies of the meadowlark, however, the mowing machine probably destroys more nests, eggs, and young birds than any other.

The parents work hard to supply their hungry babies with beetles, spiders, crickets, grubs, grasshoppers, and other insects. They never approach the nest without pausing to scan the meadow and listen for unusual sounds. If all is well, they hop to the ground, walk through the grass, and slyly

Meadowlark
3/4 life size
(10 in.)

enter the nest. Meadowlarks never fly directly from the nest unless they are frightened.

In ten days, the naked babies have turned into feathered ruffians, intent on tearing the nest apart. Sometimes they are left without a roof over their heads before they can fly. Father Meadowlark takes full charge of them until they are independent. Mother scurries about making preparations for a new family.

During the late summer and early fall, meadowlarks form small flocks and visit stubble fields and weed patches. Here they feed on grain and seeds. Many times they visit gardens and orchards to procure food. They are hardy birds; where the snowfall is light and there is bare ground most of the winter, meadowlarks are all-year residents. Where the earth is buried beneath deep snow, they migrate to the warmer climate of the South. Their bright spirits are dampened; nothing but a subdued chirp remains of the beautiful springtime song. Perhaps they are saving their voices for the time when they will return to old haunts in their beloved meadows.

Bobolink

IN THE middle of May, troops of merry minstrels descend on the fields and meadows of the northern United States and southern Canada. The Bobolink, already dressed in his mating plumage, in fine voice, and bent on telling of his recent journey from far-off Brazil and Argentina, breaks forth in rollicking song to announce his arrival.

Other North American land birds wear the darkest colors on their backs and bright colors on the breasts and underparts. The male bobolink wears his coat in topsy-turvy fashion, with a flowing white mantle over the shoulders and down the back, a buffy-yellow kerchief pushed far back on the black head, and a shiny black vest. His length is about seven inches.

For a week or more, the gay bachelor flits from weed stalk to tree limb and fills the air with ecstatic songs. Evidently he is warming up for the arrival of a buffy-brown female. Then the meadow fairly rings with a cascade of liquid music pouring from the throat of the serenader. Silvery, tinkling notes trail in the wake of his frequent courtship flights. The shy female drops to the ground and hides in the grass. But nothing dampens the ardor of Mr. Bobolink. He drops his tail, trails his wings, and puffs out his feathers in a pompous display. It would be difficult to interpret his song. One thing is sure, he announces himself by calling, *"Bob-o-link, bob-o-link,"* and adding a bright *"chink"* or *"spink."* He is little concerned that scientists call him *Dolichonyx oryzivorus*.

The little brown female builds her nest behind a screen of vegetation. It is cleverly hidden on the meadow floor and lined with a fine grass mat. Dutifully she sits on five or six grayish or buff-colored eggs, splashed with reddish-brown. While she incubates, her mate continues to sing.

Stuffed on grasshoppers, weevils, and cutworms, baby bobolinks quickly feather into mottled brown juveniles. In a month they glean weed and grass seeds with their sharp, conical bills and put on quite a show of independence.

In August, the male that was so carefree and colorful in May is reduced to a somber, brown-and-buff bird. In his fall plumage he resembles his mate and children. All that remains of his bright springtime song is a half-forgotten refrain.

A great gathering of bobolinks takes place in the fall. Western birds move eastward and mingle with larger flocks as they prepare for the return to winter homes in the southern hemisphere. Their journey of 5,000 miles is the longest undertaken by members of this family. Following ancestral flightlanes, they pass through the South, cross the Gulf of Mexico, stopping along the way to feed in grain fields and marshes, and finally reach their destination in central South America.

During the nineteenth century these flocks of bobolinks were considered a nuisance to rice farmers in the South. Sometimes they destroyed so much rice that the angry plantationers killed them by the thousands. Many of the fat little "reed birds," as they were called, were sold to city markets for eating. The carnage was so great that the bobolinks have never regained their former numbers. Now that rice growing has declined, the bobolinks are protected in all their range, for it is recognized that they destroy great numbers of harmful insects and weed seeds. Southerners and Northerners alike listen for the silvery tinkle of bells as the bobolinks wing high overhead on their nighttime migration to the pampas.

Robin

IN THE North, blustery winds still blow in February and March. The earth is covered with a blanket of snow. But a gray-coated Robin perches on a porch railing and cheerfully announces that spring is here. *"Cheerily, cheerily, cheer,"* he sings, puffing out his plump red breast.

As soon as the earth is bare, the robin begins his search for worms. Early morning is the best time to scour gardens, plowed fields, and orchards. With short, running steps, the robin crisscrosses his hunting grounds. He stops, runs, stops again, cocks his head and turns an ear to the ground—or so one would think. Really, he isn't listening; he is watching for a juicy earthworm. The robin tips forward and stabs with his bill. Sure enough, he has a worm. But the worm refuses to release its hold on the earth. It stretches and recoils. The robin pulls, backs up, and pulls again. Which will win the tug-of-war? The robin! This is the way he obtains much of his food.

Males arrive at their northern breeding grounds and are quite friendly until the females appear. Then they become ill-tempered and defend their territory and favorite female against rivals. The plucky little pugilists fly at each other like fighting cocks.

Robins love human neighbors and build their nests in the most curious places. They are found in backyard trees, on porches, beneath bridges, on steel girders of skyscrapers, and even amid the din of a railroad station.

The male is content to sing while his plain gray-brown mate does most of the hard work. He may carry bits of material, but she lays a platform of twigs, walls it with coarse grass, string, and rags, and cements it with mud. Mrs. Robin is a potter, with her own formula for adobe. Imagine how many gummy pellets of clay and mud must be carried from stream banks to plaster the walls of the nest! With wings slightly spread, she turns round and round, pushing and smoothing and shaping with her breast. A soft grass lining makes a perfect pad for the beautiful blue-green eggs—robins' egg blue, they are called.

Soon three or four naked, blind, open-mouthed babies are begging constantly for food. The parents work all day to obtain enough earthworms and

Robin
3/4 life size
(10-in.)

insects to fill the ever-hungry stomachs. There are plenty of other chores to attend to while the young birds are in the nest, too. Predators must be kept at a distance. Unwelcome guests are greeted with an outburst of cries and shrieks which alert other birds in the neighborhood. A cat is lucky to escape uninjured from the noisy, diving attacks of the angry robins. If the eggs or babies are handled by humans, the parents desert the nest and build a new one.

If there is anything robins like more than worms, it is ripe fruit. The farmer swears that the robins watch for cherries and berries to ripen, then call all the other birds to a feast. When there is an abundance of wild fruit, robins seldom do much damage to domestic crops.

Turdus migratorius, as the robin is named, is really a thrush. The English colonists who found the bird in America named it for the little red-breasted robin of the Old World, and "robin" it remains to this day. Perhaps no bird in America is so well-known to so many people. From the tree limits of Alaska and Canada to our southern borders, the sprightly robin is a familiar sight. Even in the winter a few hardy stragglers may be found sheltering in swampy woodlands or protected canyons of the North where there is sufficient food. Most of the flocks, however, move southward, where they search for worms in a milder climate and wait for spring.

Eastern Bluebird

THERE is an old tree in the orchard. The tired branches droop with age, and the trunk is wrinkled and weatherbeaten. At the base of a hollow limb, a woodpecker has drilled a hole. This hole is just the right size for a Bluebird to slip through, yet too small for a pirating starling to enter. A happy little bluebird sings to his gray-blue mate of their good fortune. From his perch in the top of the tree, the countryside unfolds before him. There are fields, gardens, woodlots, open woods with many sunny tangles, houses and lawns, and in the distance, a town. A sparkling brook divides the orchard from a meadow. What more could a bluebird ask?

Proudly the male bluebird warbles his sweetest springtime song while he guards his territory and watches his timid mate carry dry grass, bark, and leaves to line the coveted hollow. Four to six bluish-white eggs will be warm and safe within the wooden walls.

For twelve days Mother Bluebird sits on the eggs. The eggs hatch and a season of feverish activity begins. From daylight until dusk, the parents are kept busy supplying hoards of insects and bugs to hush the hunger cries. In

86

two weeks the young birds are feathered in gray with a touch of blue on the tails and wings; just a hint of the color they will be at maturity. Mottled breasts are the mark of the thrush, the family to which bluebirds belong.

When the juveniles are ready to leave the nest, the father assumes command, for the mother is already busy with preparations for a second family. Father patiently teaches his offspring to sit on a post and watch for insects on the ground, or to forage among the foliage of brushes and trees. The young birds remain with the parents through summer and fall.

Bluebirds are dainty, friendly birds, with the most gentle manners. Usually they are among the first migrants to reach their northern breeding grounds, often in the face of freezing sleet or snowstorms. Large flocks migrate by day, flying high and dropping soft, muted notes along their path. Bluebirds are among the last to leave the North in the fall. A few find shelter in swampy thickets, woods, and cedar brakes where they find sufficient food to keep them through the winter.

There are three species of bluebirds in America. *Sialia sialis,* the eastern bluebird, is the only bluebird east of the Mississippi River. This common, red-breasted bird is often called the blue robin. The western bluebird (*Sialia mexicana*) is rather common in the Pacific states. This is the bluebird with a red breast and red shoulders and blue throat. The mountain bluebird (*Sialia currucoides*) is truly a blue bird, with a blue coat and pale blue underparts shading to white on the belly. All are about seven inches long.

The lack of suitable housing accounts for a steady decline in bluebirds in many localities. Nesting boxes placed on posts and in trees meet their requirements, and those who take the time to set them up will find they have delightful summer neighbors. In return, the bluebirds will repay the favor by consuming many harmful insects and bugs, to say nothing of the musical renditions to be heard throughout the season.

Goldfinch

ALMOST everyone in the United States and Canada knows *Spinus tristis,* the Goldfinch. In some areas he is called the Wild Canary from his canarylike coloring and his outpouring of rich, trilled notes; in others, he is known as the Thistle Bird, because he feeds extensively on thistle seeds and uses the down to build his nest.

All through the sunny days of spring and early summer, flocks of these carefree songsters wing over fallow fields, bushes, hedges, and weed patches to feed on seeds and tender buds. They fly from one feeding place to another in bounding, billowing flight, like small boys on a holiday. Over the countryside the golden male spills his joyous melody. *"Chic-o-ree, chic-o-ree. Come-see-me, come-see-me."* It is easy to spot the bright songster with his small yellow body which contrasts sharply with the short, black, forked tail, black wings barred with white, a white rump, and a silken, shiny cap of black which covers his eyes.

When the purple blossoms of the thistle explode into balls of snowy down, the goldfinch knows it is time to build a nest. In July or August, after most birds have raised their families, the male goldfinch courts a plain, greenish-yellow female with pale yellow underparts and dark wings. The large flocks break up into nesting pairs, each to choose a homesite and build a nest. The nest may be on a branch of a tree, hidden in bushes, thickets, or even in dense growths of weeds, always near wild thistles or cattails.

·From the finest materials available, the female weaves a tight cup, edges it with strips of bark, and binds the fibers together with silken thread. She adds a comforter of thistledown on which to lay four to six pale blue eggs. While she attends to the eggs, her mate perches near her and sings his sweetest songs. From the trees he watches for the approach of a jay or cat. He listens for her hunger cries and takes food to the nest. After the naked hatchlings are dry and warm in their snug cradle, the parents feed them on milk from their crops. In fifteen days the lively youngsters are feathered and ready to leave the nest. Conversing in soft twittering voices, the companionable birds form flocks and continue to harvest and hull hard seeds with their stout, conical bills.

Goldfinch
actual size
(5-5½ in.)

As winter approaches, the males change their bright yellow coats for plumage of more subdued olive hues. The sharp black-and-white wings are now the only features which distinguish them from the females and immature birds. The beautiful courtship song is exchanged for a few sweet, trilled notes.

The goldfinch is a hardy bird. Even after snow falls, the little flocks continue to search for dry weed stalks. In the northern part of their range they slowly move toward the south, feeding as they go. In some places they seek shelter in the thick branches of pine trees or dense thickets and eat with other finches and redpolls.

In April and May the fearless, friendly goldfinch returns to its breeding grounds once more. Once more a golden flash is seen in trees and hedges. Once more hearts are gladdened by his lilting golden voice.

Baltimore Oriole

LIKE A flashing beacon in the sunlight, a black-and-orange bird flits through the new green foliage of trees which border village streets, streams, country lanes, or open woods. A whistle as bright and friendly as the bird himself tells the neighbors that the Baltimore Oriole has returned to his beloved summer home in the eastern part of the United States and southeastern Canada.

A few days after the male claims a tree as his territory and warns interlopers away, a female appears on the scene. She is as pretty as a picture in her greenish-orange coat and pale yellow vest. But she is drab in comparison to the male, he with the sleek black hood pulled over his head, throat, and back, the black wings touched with white bars, and the flaming reddish-orange underparts and rump. What a dashing figure he cuts as he perches beside his mate and stretches to his full height of seven and one-half inches! With a series of bows and much vigorous bobbing, he dazzles her with his brilliant colors, while he whistles a sweet love song.

His lordship chooses the tree, but it is milady that picks the very spot where the nest is to be built—a wonderful hanging pendant. Skillfully she twines string or long blades of grass about a forked twig at the end of a small branch, well above the ground. Then begins the creation of an amazing work of art. With deft strokes of her slender, sharp bill, she thrusts and pulls, shuttles and sews. Fine plant fibers, grass, string, hair, strips of paper and cloth go into the fabric forming a hanging pouch. Often she stands on her head or hangs by one foot as she ties loose ends together. As suits her fancy, she leaves an opening in the top or an entrance at the side. When the exterior is completed, she hops inside and briskly molds and shapes it with her breast while she adds a woolly lining. The finished product is an elegant silver-gray basket which gently swings in the breeze—the most elaborate creation of any North American songbird.

Mother Oriole quietly incubates four to six brown-streaked, grayish-white eggs. No one would know she was there if her mate did not sing her praises from the treetop.

Baby orioles are fed on thick liquid from the parents' bills for three days. As they grow, caterpillars, beetles, ants, boll weevils, and plant lice disappear down the hungry throats. Before long they outgrow their cozy nest, and the air is filled with cries of protest. Jays and crows are attracted by their noise, and frequently the young are lost to them.

The Baltimore oriole (*Icterus galbula*) is widely distributed over the eastern part of the United States and southeastern Canada. The bright songsters were familiar to the early colonists, who observed that these birds wore the orange and black colors of Lord Baltimore, the founder of the Maryland Colony. They named it in his honor, and it is now the state bird of Maryland.

The oriole is sometimes accused of spoiling fruit and vegetable crops, but actually he eats little vegetable matter; the damage he does is far outweighed by his destruction of boll weevils, caterpillars, grasshoppers, click beetles, and other destructive pests.

Blue Jay

CLA-CLA-CLA!" Filled with excitement and alarm, the jarring notes scream the presence of an enemy. "Beware! Beware!" the Blue Jay seems to shout as he rushes through the woods to alert birds and animals alike to the presence of a trespasser. The hue-and-cry is picked up by others of the clan, and soon the news is broadcast far and wide.

Another spirited call, *"Jay-jay-jay,"* leaves no doubt that the noisy jay has taken up a domicile in the area. The handsome blue coat, black collar, and white underparts, together with the bright blue wings and tail, both barred with black and widely fringed with white, make the blue jay (*Cyanocitta cristata*) one of our easiest birds to identify. He is our only blue-and-white bird with a crest. With the exception of Florida, he is found almost everywhere in the eastern part of the continent.

This noisy bird, full of sass and vigor, is common in parks, suburbs, and around farms. Best of all he loves open woods where both evergreens and nut-bearing trees flourish; where there is an abundance of insects, mast, and nuts to feed on.

Active, alert, and talkative, the blue jay screams and scolds as he moves from grove to grove and from thicket to branch. He delights in terrorizing smaller birds by mimicking the cry of the sharp-shinned hawk. The discovery of an owl on the roost rouses the jays to marshal their forces while they shout insults, heckle, and drive the night hunter from the woods by sheer force of numbers. From a screen of thick branches the jay takes pleasure in taunting the hawk and larger birds. But the jay himself is unpopular for his bad habit of eating the eggs and killing the young of smaller birds.

Right up to the nesting time, the blue jay bluffs and blusters. But when it is time to build the nest, he becomes quiet and furtive. Quietly the pair carry fresh twigs, strips of bark, paper, and pine needles for the loose cradle tucked away on the bough of a pine tree or in a crotch. Guarded and attended by her mate, the pretty female sits on the buff, brown-marked eggs for seventeen days.

When the youngsters are ready to leave the nest, the family wanders about,

Blue Jay
3/4 life size
(11-12 in.)

exploring the woods and searching for insects, nuts, and mast. The blue jay, so brave when shielded by a thicket, uses the utmost caution when moving across openings in the woods. One at a time the birds make the crossing, watching the while lest a circling hawk swoop down and overtake them in their slow flight. When acorns are abundant, the jay stores them beneath leaves or under the roots of trees. Like the gray squirrel, the blue jay is responsible for planting many white oak trees.

The blue jay has many calls; the sweetest is the least heard, a whispered lisping. A soft, bell-like note, *"tull-ull-ull,"* is heard in late summer when most birds are silent.

Generally, blue jays move south in the winter, yet they are residents the year around in many places in the North. As some move out of one area, others from farther north come to take their places, so the blue jay that scolded in summer may not be the same rowdy bird that is seen flashing through snow-burdened branches in winter. While he is accused of having bad manners and of robbing other birds of their eggs and young, the blue jay remains one of our most beautiful and amusing birds.

Crow

THE CROW is dressed in black from the tip of his heavy beak to the end of his sturdy toes. Far from being the dull and somber bird his apparel would lead us to believe, the crow is fairly bursting with insolence, bravado, and mischief. Some people believe he has a black heart.

To see a crowd of crows at their common assembly place is to know that they are extremely sociable. During the fall and winter, crows that breed in Canada migrate south and join their brothers in the United States. Large congregations meet at a common assembly ground and fly to roosting trees in the woods. Here they line up on limbs as though waiting to be counted. Early in the morning, powerful wings row through the air and carry the crows many miles as they forage for food. Straight as an arrow, or we might say, as the crow flies, they return in late afternoon.

"Caw, caw, caw!" A crow has spied an owl and hastens to spread the alarm. With a scream he mounts to the air and cries for other crows to join him in harassing the enemy. But often the tables are turned and the crow himself is mobbed by angry kingbirds. He may have been caught in the act of robbing a neighbor's nest, and the smaller birds want to let all the winged creatures know a thief is in the area.

Although the crow bullies and tongue-lashes other birds, he is kind and gentle to his own family. He sits on the eggs while his mate stretches her wings, and even manages to keep his voice under control so that he does not alert the hawk or owl to the whereabouts of his young ones.

The young birds are two years old when they choose a mate of their own and build a sturdy nest in the top of a woodland tree or a bush. Sticks and twigs are laid for a platform and the walls are surrounded by tangled sticks. The cup is lined with soft grass, plant fiber, and bark.

At planting time, crows flock to fields and do a great deal of damage to sprouting corn and other crops. This, with his record of depredations against chickens and young birds, has made the crow the object of "varmint hunts," poison, and bullets from the farmer's shotgun. In many places there is a bounty on his head. Various methods of ridding the country of the "pest," as the farmer calls him, have failed. Long ago, he lost the fear of scarecrows. Flying streamers and unusual noises may frighten the crow, but not for long. Curiosity soon overcomes fear and he proceeds to investigate any strange object.

One thing in the crow's favor is the fact that he destroys many harmful insects and bugs. Grasshoppers, beetles, slugs, snails, and carrion, along with berries, seeds, and vegetable matter, make up his diet.

The crow is easily tamed if taken from the nest while young, and in many instances has been taught to talk. Intelligent, amusing, and bent on carrying away any loose object that strikes his fancy, the crow can be a constant source of interest and entertainment.

The common crow *(Corvus brachyrhynchos)* is a large bird, measuring about twenty inches in length—somewhat smaller than the raven and larger than a blackbird. It is a bird of fields and woods, seldom seen in dense forests, deserts, or in high mountains. There are two other crows in America: the fish crow of the Atlantic and Gulf states, and the northwestern crow, a resident of the Pacific Northwest.

Downy Woodpecker

A SMALL, friendly, black-and-white bird makes himself at home in the woods, orchards, swampy groves, pine forests, and backyards of America. Quiet in a manner and dress, though not shy, the Downy Woodpecker is usually heard before he is seen.

Listen as he beats a tattoo on the limb of an old, dead tree. Watch as he climbs his invisible, spiral stairway up the trunk. Two toes are forward and two back. Stiff tail feathers support him as the sharp claws dig into the bark. He uses the short but powerful chisel-bill like a pile driver as he searches for grubs and worms in the wood of the tree. Coiled tendons reach from the bill to each side of the hard, thick skull. These act as shock absorbers. With his highly specialized tongue, which may be extended two inches beyond the tip of the bill, he probes into holes and burrows under the bark. One by one, the little downy woodpecker polices every tree in the orchard or woods.

In the spring, the red-capped male drums on a hollow, resounding limb or tree trunk, and accompanies his drumming with a rattling call. This attracts a female and warns other males that the territory is already taken.

The female chooses the site for her home in a partly decayed tree. The male assists her in chiseling a round hole for an entrance and hollowing out an eight-to-twelve-inch cavity for the nest. On a bed of chips and woody pulp, three to six, but usually four, white eggs are laid. For twelve days one of the adults attends them.

Downy woodpecker babies are not downy at all when they hatch, but naked and blind. Stuffed with insects all day, they make the wooden walls of their nursery buzz like a beehive before a week is over. At the age of two weeks, when they leave the dark hole, they are well-fledged.

The young birds prove to be as agile and acrobatic as the adults as they hunt industriously for coddling moths, caterpillars, wood-boring beetles, and ants. Seeds, berries, and other vegetable foods are also eaten.

During the winter, downy woodpeckers scatter through the woods and feed with chickadees, titmice, and juncos. With a soft *"peek"* note, they

Downy Woodpecker
actual size
(6½ -7 in.)

converse with their companions. Each woodpecker has his own roosting hole where he retires at night, and where he finds protection during cold winter storms. If there is a layer of powdery snow on the ground, the woodpecker dives in, and showers himself by beating his wings and throwing the snow over his back. He seems to take as much delight in this as in a water bath.

The downy woodpecker (*Dendrocopos pubescens*) is the smallest of the woodpecker clan and measures about seven inches in length. The hairy wood-pecker, a relative, looks almost exactly like him, except that he is larger. This woodpecker is less common than the downy.

Woodpeckers are never seen in flocks, but there are few wooded areas in America which do not contain at least one pair. Once they were driven from orchards and woodlots because people thought they were injurious to trees. Now it is known that the woodpecker is a friend of man and destroys insects that would otherwise destroy the trees. To attract the interesting little birds, place a bark-covered nesting box in the backyard or windbreak.

Red-winged Blackbird

FLYING with the precision of radar-controlled aircraft, thousands of Red-winged Blackbirds leave their winter homes in the South in March to wing toward northern breeding grounds. There is hardly a field, marsh, slough, or pothole in the eastern part of the United States, the Great Plains, and southern Canada that does not have its share of blackbirds in summer.

The first flights consist of males, resplendent in glossy uniforms of black. Red shoulder patches, edged with yellow or buff, glisten in the sun. They seek out their native marshes and stake their territorial claims in bulrushes and cattails. Some move on to wet meadows and bogs.

Flocks of dull, grayish-brown females, heavily streaked with sooty black, come next. They descend to the marshes and conceal themselves in the grass near the males. The males may not be ready to settle down to family life yet, and drive the females away until they are ready to mate. During the courtship the males spread their tails, ruffle the back and neck feathers, and spread the wings to display the bright red epaulets. When there is a surplus of females, the males may have two or three wives apiece. The females flutter about in the marshgrass of the male's territory and find a spot to build a nest, while the carefree males perch above them and defend their territory from other males. The colony is a noisy place, filled with chatter and song.

Yearling males arrive later. Though anxious to mate, they are shunned by the females and driven away by older males. They wander as bachelors for another year. When full grown, they measure seven to eight inches.

The nest of the red-wing is lashed to stalks of grass and reeds above the water. It is woven of wet grass, chinked with moss and mud, and lined with finer material. It takes about seven days to build and dry. Occasionally, one is placed on the ground on the bank of a sluggish stream, in bayberry bushes, or sturdy-stemmed weeds and plants.

Three to five bluish-green eggs, spotted with brown or purple, are eleven days in incubation. The babies are blind and naked when they hatch. Before they learn to fly, the young birds climb about and perch on reeds and cattails. During this time they are very vulnerable to attack, and almost half the young red-wings fall prey to mink, foxes, weasels, watersnakes, or hawks before they can wing away. The parents raise two or three broods each season.

In July, the blackbirds gather in large flocks, the males in one and the females and juveniles in another. The flocks visit farms and fallow fields where they forage for waste grain, insects, and weed seeds. The blackbirds have been accused of destroying grain crops in some areas, but actually they seem to prefer weed seeds, and they also destroy hoards of caterpillars, cankerworms, beetles, mayflies, and caddie flies in season.

Agelaius phoeniceus, the red-winged blackbird, is partially migratory. In the fall the flocks grow larger and larger in preparation for the fall southward movement. Some remain in the North all winter; others move far south or to coastal marshes, the Everglades, and rice fields. Here they forage by day in small numbers and return to the night roosts where they darken the trees and surroundings as they assemble by the thousands. They are often seen in company with grackles, starlings, and Brewer's blackbirds.

Road Runner

THERE is an amusing, picturesque bird in the Southwest not to be found elsewhere in all America. Mexicans call him *"Paisano,"* the peasant. In the mesquite and cactus country of the United States, he is known as the Roadrunner. This is a fitting title, for *Geococcyx californianus* is most often seen as he races along desert roads.

Shy and wary, yet at times bold and audacious, the roadrunner runs with his lean body and head thrust forward like a sprinter at the starting line. The long, slender tail is held horizontal or slightly down as he hotfoots across the sand on long, stout, bluish legs. Rocks and low-growing brush are mere hurdles. In and out he darts among the cactus and mesquite, and he will race an automobile at a speed up to eighteen miles an hour. Suddenly he raises his tail, using it as a brake, and comes to a halt. The race over, he darts to cover, the unkempt, heavily streaked brown-and-tan plumage fading into the landscape.

The roadrunner flies well on short, rounded wings, but he spends most of the time on the ground where he finds a variety of insects and animal food. Lizards are the chief item of his diet, perhaps because they are most abundant. Grasshoppers, crickets, beetles, mice, kangaroo rats, spiders, and other creeping things are also taken. Land snails are picked from yucca cactus and pounded against rocks until the shell cracks. Nothing is scorned. And so, in the sometimes bleak, hot, forbidding desert lands, the roadrunner ekes out a living.

The roadrunner measures as much as two feet in length, but his body is slender and always looks gaunt and undernourished. Nevertheless, this is one of the few birds with enough courage and agility to attack a rattlesnake. A rattler is coiled, vigorously shaking the rattles in warning. The roadrunner dances about, leaps into the air, and spars like a boxer warming up for a bout. The knavish yellow eye gleams fiercely beneath the rough, dark crest. A strange rasping chuckle, made by rolling the two parts of the bill together, is accompanied by the up and down, backward and forward flicking of the expressive tail. The bird always evades the rattler's deadly fangs. As the

Road Runner
1/3 life size
(20-24 in.)

snake tires, the roadrunner darts in, grasps it behind the head, shakes it viciously, and beats it on the earth until it is stunned. Not only does the roadrunner kill the snake, he eats it.

The homelife of the roadrunner is as odd as the bird himself. His nest is a large, rough structure built just above the ground in a clump of cactus or brush, and lined with feathers, grass, snakeskins, and other debris. In the nest there may be a fresh, chalky-white egg, a yellowish one just about to hatch, an ugly, black-skinned hatchling, and a feathered juvenile. The babies are fed almost entirely on lizards, which are thrust head first into their gaping mouths; sometimes they gulp and struggle but cannot swallow the whole lizard and the tail is left hanging from the mouth.

The roadrunner has a foot like the woodpecker, two toes turned forward and two back. His voice varies from a soft mew or coo to a *"squack"* as harsh as that of the jay.

Old-timers on the desert admire the picturesque and amusing bird for its ability to destroy poisonous insects and reptiles, as well as for the lively addition it makes to desert life.

Night Hawk

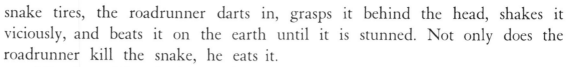

WHEN day birds are retiring, the swallowlike Nighthawk swoops over chimney tops, treetops, open woods, and fields. With long, pointed wings bent at the elbows and a slightly forked tail, he wheels, whirls, darts, and dives in the most skillful of aerial maneuvers. This is a bird of the air. He feeds on the wing, sweeping the skies of hoards of night-flying insects, moths, mosquitoes, ants, and tiny gnats. Into his cavernous mouth goes the firefly, which unwittingly tells its whereabouts with a blinking taillight. As the bird feeds, a nasal, buzzing *"peent,"* much like the voice of a woodcock, is heard.

The name of nighthawk is misleading, for this bird is not a hawk at all. Endowed with a pleasant disposition, it has weak feet and a short, soft bill, quite different from the strong talons and sharp beaks of the fierce birds of prey. The Latin name, *Chordeiles minor,* was derived from the peculiar humming which is heard when the nighthawk partly folds his wings and plummets toward the earth in a spectacular dive. This sound is made by the rush of air through the wing feathers. Just why the nighthawk makes these aerial dives—often from a height of several hundred feet—is not known. Perhaps he is in pursuit of some insect prey, or perhaps he does it just for the thrill.

The male is mottled brown and buff, with a dark back and a white throat, and white bars across the tail. The female is a more uniform brownish-buff, with a buff throat, and lacks the white tail feathers. Both have conspicuous white wing patches near the end of the wings. Their length is about nine and one-half inches.

The nighthawk has no instinct for homebuilding; the female lays her eggs in strange places which range from the flat, slate-covered roofs of city dwellings to dry streambeds and rocky slopes in fields and open woods. The two eggs are long and equally rounded on both ends. A splattering of brown and purple makes them look like the rocks among which they lie. The female sits over the eggs in a flattened position and blends inconspicuously with her surroundings.

Newly hatched babies look like flattened balls of cream-and-brown down. They are dependent on the mother for food until they can fly and forage for themselves. The mother settles by her children, outstretched wings quivering, and pumps insects into the smokey throats from her own mouth. Strong, contracting muscles enable the young birds to swallow hard-shelled bugs and large moths without chewing.

These birds are summer visitors in the United States, southeastern Alaska, and most of Canada. In the fall their graceful wings cleave the air and they migrate down the great American flyways to South America. A few remain in the southern part of the United States through the winter, but most of them wing on to Central America, Ecuador, and Colombia.

The nighthawk is a member of the Goatsucker family, about which have been woven many superstitions. Goatherds of the Old Country saw the birds as they flitted about the goats at night and thought they must be sucking their blood. Instead, the birds were feeding on insects which swarmed around the animals. The nighthawk is also called will-o'-the-wisp, and is often mistaken for the whippoorwill, a bird of similar coloring and night habits. The nighthawk can be distinguished, however, by his white wing bars.

Ruby-throated Hummingbird

THE RUBY-THROATED HUMMINGBIRD is one of our most remarkable birds, a never-ending source of wonder and interest. The family of the hummingbird constitutes the smallest birds in America, and they are found only in the Americas. They build the smallest nests, lay the smallest eggs, have the fastest heartbeats and wingbeats, and are veritable flying dynamos.

The ruby-throated hummingbird *(Archilorus colubris)* weighs only one-eighth of an ounce and is three and one-half inches long. This is the most widely distributed hummingbird in the eastern United States and Canada, and breeds only east of the Rocky Mountains. In the spring and fall migration, some of these little travelers make a journey from Central America to southern Canada, a distance of more than 2,000 miles. Some come by way of Mexico; others scorn the overland route and fly directly across the Gulf of Mexico, a nonstop flight of 500 miles. Before leaving on the journey, they store up extra fat to use as a reserve fuel supply. When they reach their destination, they weigh only as much as a copper cent.

In the United States, they move north as fast as their favorite flowers burst into bloom. The males reach their breeding grounds first and establish a territory which they pugnaciously defend against all trespassers. Dressed in exquisite plumage of glossy metallic green, with a bright red throat, the males display the magic of their flight before the females, who arrive later. Swinging like a pendulum in a U-shaped arc, their wings beat at a speed of fifty to seventy times a second. Their hearts race up to 615 times a minute. Each bird consumes twice its weight in food every day to replace the energy lost in constant flight.

The male leaves to his mate the task of building the nest and rearing the young. The nest is as tiny as the bird. It is no larger than a quarter, and about an inch in depth. Walled with delicate bud scales, covered with gray lichens, lined with down, and bound to a limb with silken spiderweb, which are held in place with sticky saliva, it resembles a knot on a limb. Here the female lays two pea-sized eggs, precious as two white pearls, and so small it would take 5,000 to equal the weight of an ostrich egg.

Ruby-throated Hummingbird
1/4 over life size
(3¼ in.)

Laden with a cargo of nectar, the mother returns to feed the young on an average of five times an hour. She thrusts her long, needle-shaped bill into the open mouths and pumps them full of sweets. In three weeks the babies are fledged and their powers of flight well developed. They leave the nest to syphon their own food supply from bright-colored flowers in gardens, fields, and open woods. Their tubular tongues are perfect sipping straws with which to tap the nectar pots, as well as to catch small insects which loiter in the hearts of the flowers.

The young birds resemble the female, with her green back and dull-white underparts. All females have white in the wing feathers, and all humming-birds have small, weak feet, little adapted for walking. But then, birds with such marvelous powers of flight have little need to walk. They zoom up and down and sideways, or fly in reverse, supported by two gossamer clouds of humming wings. A variety of sharp, highpitched notes and short syllables are voiced as they flit from one flower to another.

Hummingbirds can escape from bird enemies, but killing frosts often destroy the blossoms, and with them, the birds' source of food. Sleet, hail, and winds are also frequent causes of death. Yet despite the hazards of migration and the elements, the hummingbirds continue to visit our gardens and seem to be as numerous as ever.

House Wren

THERE comes to our yards and fields in April and May a little brown bird called the House Wren. He arrives at his favorite northern breeding territory and stakes a claim in roadside trees, bushes, garden shrubs, and along the fringe of wooded meadows. Bursting with energy, the male pours forth a loud, bubbling torrent of liquid notes, which serves to notify other birds that they are trespassing on his domain. If intruders are not intimidated by his oft-repeated refrain, he resorts to scolding and threats. When all else fails, the pugnacious little fighter, though only five inches long, attacks with force.

The house wren lays no claim to fine feathers. In fact, he is quite a drab bird with a brown coat, barred wings and tail, and buff underparts. What he lacks in color, however, he makes up for in a display of boundless energy. Nervous and fidgety, he is seldom quiet for a moment. The tail, narrow and rounded on the end, reflects his mood, perched high or energetically flicking from side to side, or falling down in dejection.

While the male waits for a female to arrive, he devotes himself to building numerous nests, all of which he leaves unfinished. And he chooses the strangest places to build them. He stuffs twigs and grass into tin cans, woodpecker holes, mailboxes, discarded shoes, porch niches, and even the skulls of dead animals. Nesting boxes in backyards are especially attractive to the little builder, and much more so if they have small holes to discourage sparrows. The wren often dislodges other birds from his nest.

The male pays court with his wings aquiver and his tail standing straight up. If the female accepts his advances, she may choose one of the unfinished nests the male started to build. Many times, though, she scorns his efforts, tears the half-finished nest apart, and rebuilds it to her satisfaction.

Six to eight eggs, sprinkled with fine reddish-brown dots, hatch in about thirteen days. Wrens have strong feeding instincts, and these babies receive the very best of care. Many times unattached birds are seen feeding the young of other species. The young wrens soon scatter through the underbrush and shrubs searching for grasshoppers, beetles, and other insects. The wren family destroys many harmful bugs during the course of a single summer.

Far from being a model of domestic bliss, a pair of wrens bicker and quarrel all through the nesting period. Jenny Wren, as she is sometimes called. fusses and scolds at her lively mate, but he continues to sing as merrily as if he hadn't a care in the world. The male often takes another wife, and the first one retires to another nest to raise a second family.

When autumn winds whisper of colder days to come, the house wrens desert yards and farms and flock in the woods where they make preparations for the southward journey. Flocks from southern Canada and the northern part of the United States move to the Gulf of Mexico, Baja California, and the coasts of Mexico. Some stay in the South all the year round.

Troglodytes aedon is the imposing scientific name of the house wren, which is the best known of several species in the United States. Others are the cactus wren and rock wren of the Southwest, the Carolina wren of the Southeast, and the marsh wren.

Barn Swallow

EVERYONE in rural North America knows the Barn Swallow. These sleek, beautiful birds, with blue-black backs, chestnut breasts and foreheads, saber-like wings and long, forked tails skim gracefully over towns, farms, and open woods as they scour the skies for flying insects. They can be seen feeding near ponds in the twilight hours and on moonlight nights.

The barn swallow was so named because of his fondness for building his nest on the eaves and rafters of old-fashioned barns, to which he faithfully returns summer after summer. Originally, of course, these swallows nested in natural cavities, in caves and holes. As farming spread, the swallows found barns and farm buildings more to their liking since they offered better protection from the elements, and they became almost as domesticated as the barnyard fowls. Today modern barns, with their tight-fitting doors, offer little hospitality to the barn swallow, but fortunately there are still many old buildings which afford good nesting spots.

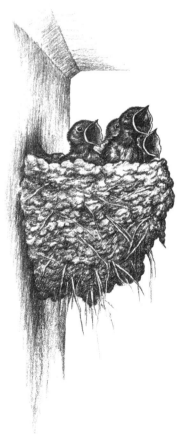

In the spring, barn swallows make the long journey from South America to the United States, Canada, and even northern Alaska. They fly in flocks, wheeling high over the countryside and avoiding large bodies of water. Their flight is swift, so swift the hawk is easily outdistanced. At night they stop to rest and feed. Their call is a twittering note, prolonged and joyful. As they fly, a soft *"kvit-kvit-wit-wit,"* not really a song, but pleasing to the ear, is heard.

Females and immature birds look alike with only a warm blush on the breasts. The bills are small and the mouths large for trapping insects. The feet are small and weak, fine for perching, but ill adapted for running on the ground.

Courting birds lock bills much as young lovers hold hands. Gently each combs the plumage of the other. Devoted and kind, the male shares the house-building tasks and care of the young.

From the banks of ponds and streams, the swallows carry mud balls and tamp them in place with their bills to make a bowl-shaped nest, attached to barn timbers or the sides of caves. In the barnyards the birds find a good supply

Barn Swallow
actual size
(6-7½ in.)

of straw with which to reinforce the walls. Often five or six pair have adjacent nests. When the nests are dry and lined with feathers and animal hair, the female lays four to six white eggs spotted with reddish-brown.

The baby swallows are rather ugly and sparsely covered with down, but in a few weeks they are transformed into handsome young birds. The parents tempt them to leave the mud houses by flying back and forth in front of them with insects in their mouths. Father guards and trains them while Mother lays more eggs. The juveniles often help feed the second brood.

Family ties are strong. As summer wanes, the swallows form large flocks and move to coastal marshes where they feed for a few weeks before leaving for their winter homes in the South.

Hirundo rustica, the barn swallow, is also called the Mud Dauber, not a very colorful name for a bird that is so handsome in appearance and so graceful in flight.

Purple Martin

AMONG our American birds we have an apartment dweller—one that has lived in bird houses so long that only in a few places do they still build homes of their own. The Indians of pre-colonial days started the custom. In their cornfields they hung hollow gourds with a hole in the side for the birds to enter. Purple Martins moved in and drove crows and other crop-destroying birds away. The practice was adopted by the southern planters, and soon the idea spread. Today tens of thousands of purple martins occupy housing provided by farmers, townsmen, and city dwellers. The martins are most common in the eastern half of the continent; they are rare in the West.

The purple martin (*Progne subis*) is the largest of our swallows, measuring seven inches in length. It is the only American swallow to be completely dark. The males have blue-black backs and heads which shine richly purple, and the underparts are dark. The females, immature birds, and first-year males have lighter underparts and a grayish cast to the feathers, but the purple is there.

In January, the first martins begin to appear in the southern states from their winter homes in South and Central America. It may be April when the last migrants reach Canada. Young males come first and battle fiercely for a place in one of the numerous housing projects. It might be the one in which they had been hatched. The females, unattached, come next, and the males vie for a mate. No sooner are they settled in their apartment than old couples, mated before they arrive, come and thrust the young couples out of the choicest nesting places. When all the housing difficulties are settled, the birds live together in harmony.

With any building material the surroundings afford, such as rags, straw, grass, leaves, and other debris, the birds build a nest in the house provided for them and place a dirt barrier at the entrance to keep the five eggs from rolling out. In two weeks the baby martins hatch. It would seem that with so many parents on the wing, sweeping the skies for insects, the supply would soon be depleted, but they find plenty for their own needs and their children, too. A low, rolling twitter accompanies their feeding flight as they skim through the skies. They are adept at plucking insects from the top of waving grass and at bathing on the wing. They fly low over a pool, dip their tails in the water and spray it all over them, then rise and shake vigorously to send another spray through the air. Fearlessly, they drive crows and hawks from their territory. Their chief enemies are the English sparrow and the starling, which sometimes force them out of their homes.

Frost and snow or sleet storms are to be dreaded, since the cold kills the insects on which the martins feed. In a week many of the birds can die from lack of food. Excessive summer heat sometimes kills the nestlings.

The purple martins leave their nesting places in August and September to forage and roost in flocks. Trees in city parks as well as wooded country areas are often black with the birds. Thousands move toward the coast, where they feed over the salt marshes before leaving on their southward journey.

In sparsely settled areas where the birds do not find ready-made nesting facilities, a few pair may find homes in woodpecker holes or rotting trees. Most of them will return to the same sites each spring to fill the skies with graceful flights and the bird houses with homemaking activities.

Index